THE GIANTS

**MEMORIES AND
MEMORABILIA
FROM A CENTURY
OF BASEBALL**

Text by Bruce Chadwick
Photography by David M. Spindel

ABBEVILLE PRESS · PUBLISHERS
New York · London · Paris

CONTENTS

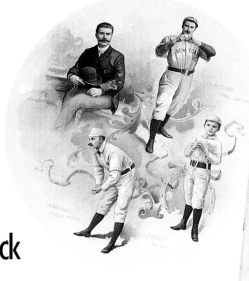

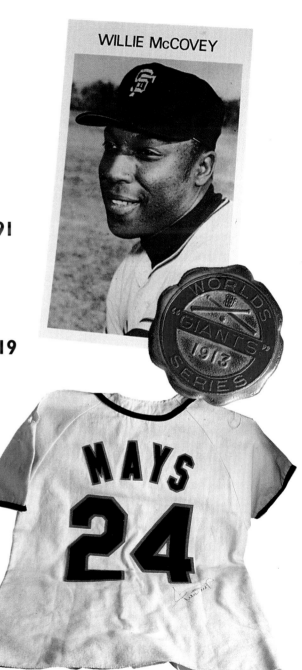

To Margie and Rory.

—B.C.

EDITOR: Constance Herndon
DESIGNERS: Barbara Balch and Patricia Fabricant
PRODUCTION EDITOR: Sarah Key
PRODUCTION MANAGER: Simone René

To my mentors, Ralph Hattersley, Tosh Matsomato, and Dr. Richard Zakia, for encouraging me to fulfill my creative dreams.

—D.S.

Library of Congress Cataloging-in-Publication Data
Chadwick, Bruce
    The Giants: memories and memorabilia from a century of baseball/
    by Bruce Chadwick, photography by David Spindel.
        p.   cm.
    ISBN 1-55859-379-9
    1. New York Giants (baseball team)—History. 2. San Francisco Giants (baseball team)—History. I. Spindel, David. II. Title.
GV875.N42C47   1993
796.357'64'097471—dc20   92-32272
                                        CIP

Page 1: Giants pennants, East and West (see p. 92); pages 2-3: the Giants, 1913 (p. 38); frontispiece: Giants' memorabilia through the years; page 5: ball signed by Dravecky, Mitchell, Clark, et al. (p. 138); title page, left to right: Mathewson ad piece (p. 26), San Francisco Giants button (p. 126), page from early Giants book (p. 18); Kevin Mitchell's cap (p. 140); program from 1917 Series (p. 39); McCovey card (p. 98); press pin from 1913 Series (pg. 36); Mays's jersey (p. 84).

Front cover, from upper left: Monte Irvin and teammates celebrate 1951 Series win over Yankees (p. 73), 1917 Series ribbon (p. 39), Mays button (p. 72), San Franciso flag (p. 102), Giants bobbin' head doll (p. 133), Giants line-up, 1912 (p. 32).

Back cover, clockwise from upper right: Giants celebrate 1962 pennant win over Dodgers (p. 111), stamp book (p. 72), ball from 1922 Series win over Yankees (p. 47), McCovey glove (p. 123), Durocher arguing the fine points (p. 74), Mathewson souvenir fan (p. 34), ticket from Giants' tour of Japan, 1953 (p. 81).

ACKNOWLEDGMENTS

We'd like to thank the dozens of collectors and fans, both kids and adults, who talked to us about their baseball collections and let us photograph their memorabilia at stores, museums, card shows, and stadiums. We are particularly grateful to Duane Garrett of San Francisco, "Mr. Giants," who let us photograph his vast and wonderful collection, and to Len Farber of New York. Thanks also to Josh Evans, president of Lelands, Inc., the New York sports auction house, for his assistance, and to the hard-working researchers at the National Baseball Hall of Fame in Cooperstown, particularly its photo director, Patricia Kelly.

In addition, we'd like to express our appreciation to Bob Lurie and the staff of the San Francisco Giants for their enthusiastic cooperation. The athletes and sports personalities who talked to us were also helpful, particularly Willie Mays, Monte Irvin, Will Clark, Dusty Baker, Matt Williams, Johnny Mize, and the late Leo Durocher.

Finally, our special thanks to Constance Herndon, our editor, and Patricia Fabricant and Barbara Balch, our designers, who worked with us to turn a good book into a great one.

BRUCE CHADWICK AND DAVID M. SPINDEL

FROM COOGAN'S BLUFF TO CANDLESTICK

The numbers are impressive enough. Over the course of 109 years in the National League, first in New York and then in San Francisco, the Giants have won sixteen pennants and five world championships. Fans say that in baseball, a sport mired in statistics, the numbers tell the story. Actually, numbers rarely tell the story in sports. That's certainly true with the Giants—the numbers only tell half of it.

Giants pennants through the ages.

Only the Brooklyn Dodgers, who desegregated the game, have had more effect on baseball in America than the Giants. But the Giants made their impact without being first in anything in the major leagues. They weren't the first professional team in the majors and they weren't even among the first teams in the National League (they joined seven years later, in 1883). They weren't the first pro club in New York (a team called the Mutuals was). They didn't win the first World Series or the most World Series or even the most pennants.

But it was the Giants who established professional baseball as the king of sports in the 1880s, a time when the nation was top-heavy with sports, and their success opened the door for the Dodgers and Yankees. It was the Giants who dominated all of baseball in the early years of the twentieth century, when baseball had to fend off boxing, college football, and even six-day bike races for the consumer dollar. It was the managerial

11

pitching phenom, who transformed the game from one played by ruffians to one also played by college graduates, and in so doing, broadened its box-office appeal to women and children, truly making it a sport for all.

The Giants also gave baseball a never-to-be-forgotten shot of adrenalin, a moment that transcended the sport itself, with their incredible come-from-behind pennant run in 1951, a series topped off by Bobby Thomson's astonishing home run known as "the shot heard 'round the world." And it was the Giants who found a kid named Willie Mays, just a teenager, then playing in the Negro Leagues, and brought him up to the majors to give America one of its most spectacular sports heroes.

Finally, it was the Giants, along with the Dodgers, who brought baseball to California in 1958. Loyal fans in New York hated them for it, but the move made baseball a truly national game, not just a game played between the Atlantic seaboard and the Mississippi River. The move to California completed the dreams of Abner Doubleday, Henry Chadwick, Alexander Cartwright, Rube Foster, and other pioneers of the game, men who believed that baseball would one day be played coast to coast, in front of men, women, and especially children of all colors and all nationalities.

Like the Dodgers and Yankees, the Giants never hurt for programs, yearbooks, stamp books, pins, and pennants.

genius of the Giants' John McGraw that made the game a manager's game, not a players' game as it had been in the 1800s. It was the college-educated and sophisticated Christy Mathewson, the great Giants

One corner of San Francisco collector Duane Garrett's treasure room. His Polo Grounds chair is surrounded by catchers' gear and bats along with gloves and balls signed by more than 100 players over the years, all the way back to 1884.

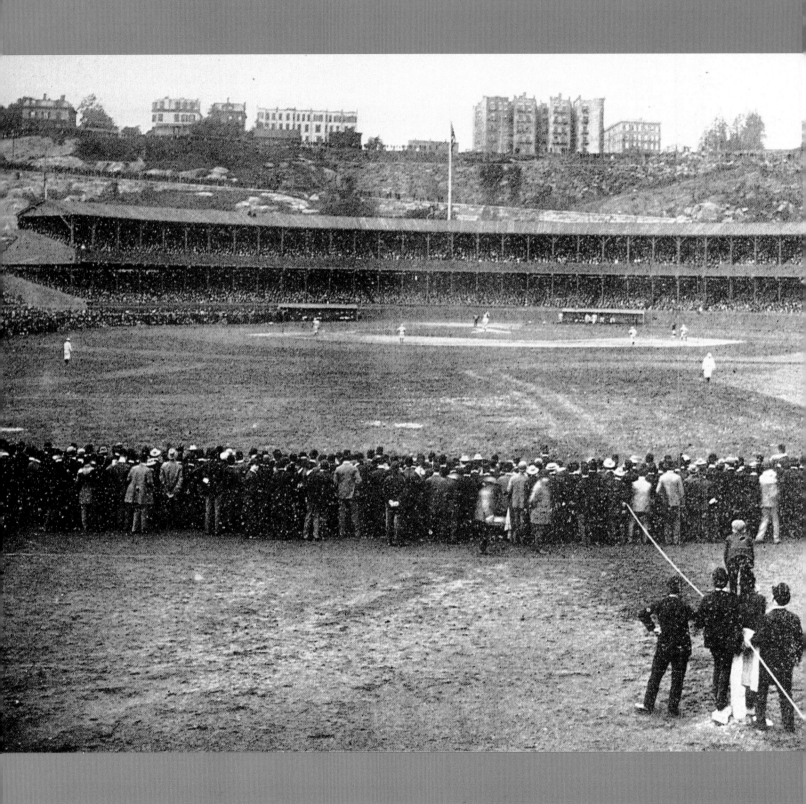

CHAPTER ONE

MORE THAN POLO AT THE POLO GROUNDS

1880s to 1902

Midway through the explosive nineteenth century, the game of baseball was thriving in bustling, booming New York, capital city of America's Industrial Revolution and jumping-off point for millions of immigrants. There were over a hundred different amateur baseball teams—factory workers, ethnic squads, and gentlemen's clubs. During the Civil War the armies took up the game and, when the war was over, baseball's popularity spread across the country with the returning troops. Soon team and field owners were charging money and making tidy profits off the game. America being what it is, entrepreneurs quickly spotted a chance to make a small fortune. But what was really needed was some kind of organization that would allow teams from different cities to play each other on a regular basis and develop profitable intercity rivalries. The answer, ultimately, was the National League of Professional Base Ball Clubs, formed at New York's Gotham Hotel in 1876, which initially included clubs from Chicago, St. Louis, Louisville, Cincinnati, Hartford, Boston, Philadelphia, and New York.

New York's first team, the Mutuals, was owned by Bill Cammeyer, a Brooklyn businessman, but it only lasted in the league for a single season. Realizing that a late-season road trip would cost him too much money, Cammeyer canceled it, so William Hulbert, the first president of the new

When regular seats for a game were sold out, turn-of-the-century owners gleefully sold standing-room tickets to fans, who watched the game standing in the outfield. As this 1901 photo of a game at the Polo Grounds shows, a good many more tickets could be sold this way, from 3,000 to 5,000. As for the technical problems posed by the arrangement, fly balls hit into fans on the outfield grass were considered ground-rule doubles.

15

As this 1888 score-card shows, slugger Roger Connor was hitting third for the Giants that season. He held the career home run record (131) until Babe Ruth broke it, and became the first man to hit three home runs in one game. These 1880s scorecards are particularly rare pieces of memorabilia today because they were printed on thick cardboard and were easily bent or destroyed.

National League, kicked the Mutuals out. After all, Hulbert reasoned, with his league so popular, who needed New York? Well, as it turned out, everybody did (then and now). The league wasn't generating enough revenue without a New York City entry, and the natural rivalries that were Hulbert's dream simply didn't work with teams like Troy and Buffalo in and New York and Philadelphia out.

Right around this time two wealthy New York fans named Jim Mutrie and John B. Day formed their own team, the Metropolitans. They were going to lease a field in New Jersey until someone told them about one on the upper east side of Manhattan that was currently used for polo matches. The owners snapped up the lease, installed wooden grandstand seating for several thousand spectators, and called their field, for want of a better name, "the Polo Grounds." The Metropolitans played a 24-game season against independents in 1880 and 151 games the next year against independents, colleges, and National

This heavy, thick-handled bat was standard issue in the National League during the 1880s.

J. U. STEAD,   383 6th Ave., N. Y.

Mowbray   2338 EIGHTH AVENUE
NEW YORK

Collected and displayed by early baseball fans, these 4 x 6-inch sepia photos were called "cabinet" cards because they were displayed in cabinets. Three are unknown players, but the gent with the long drooping moustache is Al Whitney.

League teams in exhibitions. By 1883 the team had gained admittance into the upstart American Association, and in 1884 they won the league's pennant.

Meanwhile, Day and Mutrie were developing a second New York team, the Gothams, which entered the National League. When Mutrie took over management of the Gothams in 1885, he beefed up the team with some of his pennant-winning Metropolitans. In fact the club got

so good it won 85 of its 112 games that year (just two shy of the pennant-winning Chicago White Stockings), and, in the process, earned itself a new name. After a particularly satisfying June 3 victory over Philadelphia, so the story is told, Mutrie was struggling to find words to describe his triumphant players. "Look at them," he spluttered, "they're . . . they're . . . *Giants!*" Thus was bestowed the name that has adorned sports history for over a century.

In the 1880s, fans collected thin, 9-inch-diameter books with illustrations of players. Gracing this page (*counterclockwise from top left*) are infielder Jim O'Rourke, second baseman Hardy Richardson, home run king Roger Connor, and center fielder George Gore.

They were giant characters, too, the stuff of dime novels as well as sports pages. The Giants were loaded with great players in the early years, men who would spend eternity in Cooperstown. Roger Connor, who had come down from Troy, was the league's most feared slugger. He packed 220 pounds of brawn on his frame and used it to hit 136 home runs, including three in one game—a record that would stand until Babe Ruth broke it in the lively ball era. In addition to Connor, Mickey

Owner/manager Jim Mutrie (*in suit*) highlights the right page, along with pitcher Cannonball Titcomb (*upper right*), third sacker Albert Whitney (*lower left*), and the Giants mascot, ten-year-old Willie Breslin, who appeared in all team pictures of the era.

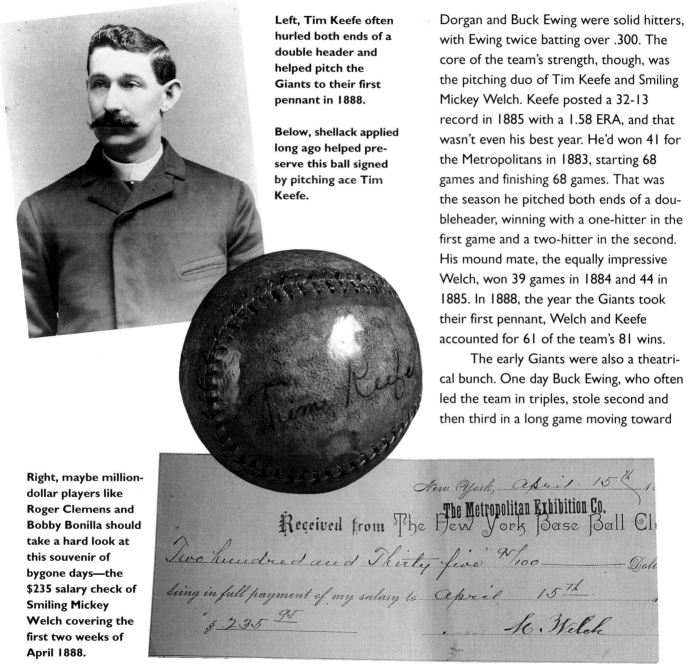

Left, Tim Keefe often hurled both ends of a double header and helped pitch the Giants to their first pennant in 1888.

Below, shellack applied long ago helped preserve this ball signed by pitching ace Tim Keefe.

Right, maybe million-dollar players like Roger Clemens and Bobby Bonilla should take a hard look at this souvenir of bygone days—the $235 salary check of Smiling Mickey Welch covering the first two weeks of April 1888.

Dorgan and Buck Ewing were solid hitters, with Ewing twice batting over .300. The core of the team's strength, though, was the pitching duo of Tim Keefe and Smiling Mickey Welch. Keefe posted a 32-13 record in 1885 with a 1.58 ERA, and that wasn't even his best year. He'd won 41 for the Metropolitans in 1883, starting 68 games and finishing 68 games. That was the season he pitched both ends of a doubleheader, winning with a one-hitter in the first game and a two-hitter in the second. His mound mate, the equally impressive Welch, won 39 games in 1884 and 44 in 1885. In 1888, the year the Giants took their first pennant, Welch and Keefe accounted for 61 of the team's 81 wins.

The early Giants were also a theatrical bunch. One day Buck Ewing, who often led the team in triples, stole second and then third in a long game moving toward

New York, April 15th 1

The Metropolitan Exhibition Co.

Received from The New York Base Ball Clu

Two hundred and Thirty five N/100 ———— Doll

being in full payment of my salary to April 15th

$235 95

M. Welch

The original Polo Grounds, which burned down in 1911, with fan watching from carriages.

darkness. At third he turned to the crowd, cupped his hands, and shouted, "It's getting late. I'm going to steal home and then we can all have dinner." And, on the next pitch, he did.

Shortstop John Montgomery Ward, a practicing lawyer and the team's intellectual, led hundreds of players out of the National League in 1890 over a salary dispute and formed the short-lived ballplayer-controlled Players' League. Monte Ward also took great delight in suing and beating owners in player contract disputes.

Jim Mutrie, the snappily dressed co-owner of the Giants, was also the team's cheerleader. He would skip up and down the aisles of the stands and start his traditional cheer by shouting to a group of spectators, "Who are the people?" They would roar back, "We are the people!" Then

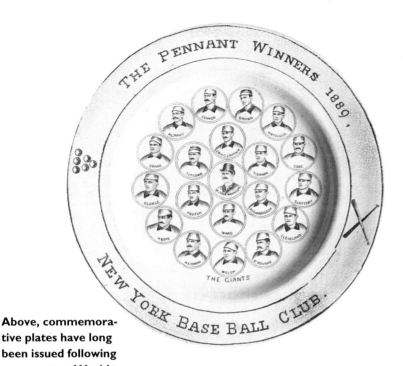

Above, commemorative plates have long been issued following a pennant or World Series. This beautiful 1889 Giants plate, picturing every player and the manager, was one of the first.

Mutrie, in his best Toscanini, would lead them in the Giants' fight song, "We are the People."

Their talents and antics made crowd-pleasers of the Giants, who built a new, larger Polo Grounds at 159th Street beneath Coogan's Bluff on the Harlem River. They played very well, winning back-to-back National League pennants in 1888 and 1889. But in 1890, the year of the Players' League, the Giants suddenly found themselves in a Keystone Kops movie.

Several of the top Giants stars bolted for Players' clubs. Monte Ward, the leader of the League, went to Brooklyn, but Connor, Keefe, Ewing, and several others joined the Manhattan entry. The new club built its stadium right next to the Polo Grounds, scheduled its games at the same time, and—in a final galling blow—named

Rare and in mint condition, this 12 x 8-inch cardboard cutout depicts a typical 1890s New York City horse-drawn trolley adorned with ads for the Polo Grounds and that day's game.

21

its team the Giants! The two stadiums were so close that fans in one could watch part of the game in the other, and hawkers outside sold tickets to both. Confusion reigned. One day a player actually hit a home run over the center-field fence of the Polo Grounds that smashed into the back wall of the Players' League park, where a game was in progress. He got an ovation from fans in both parks as he rounded the bases for the only home run hit in two ball-parks simultaneously.

The upstart Players' League was not well financed, however, and lasted just one season, so when it folded many of the rebel Giants came back to the *real* Giants (having convinced the owners to drop their new salary structure). By 1894 the club, now managed by Monte Ward, had rebounded. But after Andrew Freedman purchased it in 1895, it slumped through the rest of the decade. Freedman, who feuded with other owners, the press, and his own players (trying to sue several), fired twelve managers in eight years and ran the club into the ground. He finally left baseball in 1902 and sold the Giants to minority owner John T. Brush, who found he had a club with few stars, few fans, and little press support. One thing he did have, however, was Freedman's twelfth and finest manager, John McGraw.

This scorecard is not from the National League's Giants but rather from another team of the same name that belonged to the upstart Players League. Formed in 1890 to protest what many players saw as their exploitation by club owners, the new league lasted just one season. Their New York team badly undermined the National League Giants by signing a number of their players and building a field right next to the Polo Grounds.

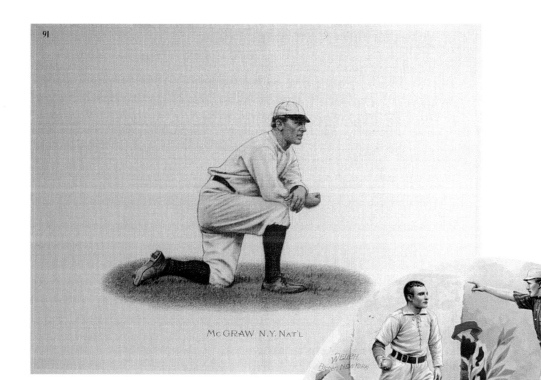

McGRAW N.Y. NAT'L

Below, another page from the Giants book, featuring (*counterclockwise from upper left*) pitcher Smiling Mickey Welch, team captain Buck Ewing, pitcher Tim Keefe, and Monte Ward, shortstop and founder of the renegade Players League.

Above, at the turn of the century, manufacturers made "silks," as these thin silk flags were called, with famous ballplayers on them. This one features John McGraw.

CHAPTER TWO

THE McGRAW ERA

1902–1932

efore he turned to managing, John McGraw had been a feisty third baseman with the National League's Baltimore Orioles, a powerhouse that won three straight titles from 1894 to 1896. Nobody had intimidated John McGraw, who frequently blocked, pushed, and tripped runners on the base paths. He wouldn't let the game's managers intimidate him either, and in 1899 when the Baltimore owners tried to send him North with a group of Oriole starters to beef up their Brooklyn club, McGraw refused to go.

Ironically, it was in New York that McGraw would become famous. But before then he turned to managing, with the Orioles, played for St. Louis, and then returned to Baltimore in 1901 to manage again. After a year and half, McGraw took the plunge that would make him one of baseball's greatest legends. It was mid-season 1902 when he moved to New York to manage the hapless Giants. Nobody's fool, McGraw pulled some strings and arranged to bring Dan McGann, Roger Bresnahan, and Iron Man Joe McGinnity with him from Baltimore.

The team he found in New York had the makings of a dynasty and he knew it. He had decent hitters in George Browne and Billy Lauder, and a good rotation pitcher in Luther "Dummy" Taylor, a deaf-mute. But the jewel in the crown, of course, was the great pitcher Christy Mathewson,

John McGraw *(left)* managed the Giants for 29 years and took them to first- or second-place finishes 21 times, often with ace hurler Christy Mathewson *(right)* .

A finely detailed advertising broadside for cigarettes proclaiming Mathewson the "World's Greatest Pitcher." For once, there was no exaggeration.

who would startle the country by winning 30 games or more in each of McGraw's first three seasons with the Giants.

McGraw was a rough, aggressive manager who angered the crowds in every city. He constantly argued with umpires, players, and other managers. He argued with fans. He argued with people in the lobbies of hotels across the country. He was loud, he was volatile, and sometimes he seemed close to bursting out of his chunky frame as his round, rugged face turned ever deeper shades of red.

But he was also a man who went along with the religious Mathewson's wish never to pitch on Sunday. McGraw saw nothing wrong with that and simply juggled the rotation to accommodate his star pitcher. He also found no fault, as others did, with Mathewson's obsession with

checkers. Matty played so well that he was the unquestioned national champion and would often take on six opponents at the same time, just for practice. He would play three straight hours on the morning of a game, explaining to McGraw that checkers helped him sharpen his concentration for the game. McGraw, remembering Matty's 30-win seasons, went along.

The hard-nosed McGraw had one problem on his hands right from the start—what to do with Dummy Taylor, the only deaf-mute to play in the big leagues in the twentieth century. Taylor, half-serious, half-clown, couldn't communicate with anyone on the team because no one knew sign language. A talented pitcher, he was alone and miserable. The easy thing to do was to trade him, but McGraw felt bad for him and decided to have every single one

This extremely rare 1905 World Series program featured the Giants on its cover. During the Series, Mathewson hurled an unprecedented three consecutive shutouts, a feat unmatched before or since.

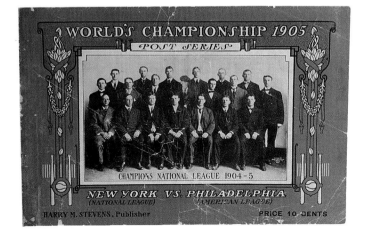

LUTHER H. TAYLOR
PITCHER OF THE NEW YORK (N. L.) CLUB

Luther "Dummy" Taylor, the only deaf mute to play in the majors in this century, won 21 games for the Giants in 1904. So that Taylor's teammates could communicate with him, McGraw had the entire club learn sign language, the gestures of which became the earliest form of baseball signs.

As McGraw's fame grew, so did the size of his autograph.

of the Giants go to a school for the deaf and learn sign language. Never one to waste effort, McGraw then used the sign language everyone knew so well to deliver messages, via flying fingers, to pitchers, catchers, and baserunners. It was the first time "signs" were used in the game.

McGraw also attempted to integrate baseball by trying to sign a black second baseman named Charlie Grant who was playing on an all-black team. The manager told people that Grant was really a full-blooded Cherokee named Charlie Tokohama, but the other owners didn't buy it. McGraw could be something of a senti-mentalist, although generally with practical results. Near the end of the 1904 season, the year McGraw won his first pennant, he heard that a local 52-year-old attorney named Jim O'Rourke longed to play base-ball one last time. O'Rourke, a future Hall of Famer, had been a great player in the 1880s and had, in fact, smashed the very first hit in major league history in 1876. Touched by O'Rourke's whimsy, McGraw had him suit up and catch on September 22, 1904, a game in which victory would clinch the pennant. The aging attorney shoved his gray hair under a catcher's mask, caught all nine innings, and went 1-for-4 at the plate, even scoring a run. The final score: Giants 7, Cincinnati 5. McGraw the softie had struck again.

27

Exasperated with his club, Giants' owner John Brush (below) hired John "Muggsy" McGraw from Baltimore and changed the face of New York baseball. The entrepreneur, who made his money in department stores, refused to participate in the 1904 World Series with his National League champion Giants, charging that the three-year-old American League was little more than a minor league.

McGraw was often the center of controversy. In 1904 he and Giants owner John Brush decided that if they won the pennant they would not play in the newly inaugurated World Series as Boston and Pittsburgh had in 1903. The American League, now just four years old, was really nothing more than minor league ball, they maintained. The 1904 team, one of the Giants' greatest, won the pennant and stuck to their word, snubbing the furious American League champion Red Sox.

The following year McGraw and Brush relented and the Giants played the Philadelphia A's for the world championship. In this series, which the Giants took four games to one, Mathewson put on

perhaps the greatest pitching performance in major league history, hurling three consecutive shutouts, striking out 18 batters, and giving up just 14 hits and one walk. Nothing like it has been done since.

That was the start of the McGraw era, one that would span 29 seasons and several generations. When it began, neither the airplane nor the car had been invented; at its end, Lindbergh's transatlantic flight was five-year-old history and auto racing had become a popular sport. While six U.S. presidents came and went, McGraw's Giants towered over baseball, finishing first or second in 21 of 29 years and taking home ten pennants and three world championships.

The Giants' 1906 season pass glorified the previous year's World Series champs.

28

The 1904 Giants team, shown here on the cover of *Sporting Life*, won the pennant but refused to play the Boston Red Sox in what would have been the second World Series.

This cracked bat was used by Fred Merkle, a young Giant whose dramatic if dim-witted error lost a crucial game to the Cubs in 1908.

Hard Luck Fred Merkle.

It was one of the years the Giants finished second that will live in infamy—the year a journeyman ballplayer named Fred Merkle became immortal the wrong way. On September 23, 1908, the Giants and the Chicago Cubs were battling for first place when they met at a packed Polo Grounds. In the bottom of the ninth, the Giants' Al Bridwell singled home Moose McCormick for the win, but rookie Merkle, who had been on first, failed to touch the bag at second to end the game. Assuming the game had ended when McCormick crossed home plate, he turned and ran to the clubhouse as thousands of delighted fans swarmed onto the field. But the Cubs called for the ball and tagged sec-

ond, claiming a forceout. When the umpire ruled the game a tie, fans rioted, pelting the field with seat cushions. Legal maneuvering followed, but league president Harry Pulliam stood by the 1-1 tie. At the end of the season the Giants and Cubs were tied for first in the standings and the Cubs beat the Giants in a one-game playoff. Merkle's boneheaded play had cost them the pennant. Pulliam, unable to deal with the controversy over his decision, committed suicide the next year.

Despite the occasional monumental error like Merkle's, there was great talent on those Giants teams. Iron Man Joe McGinnity, who often pitched both ends of a doubleheader, once won five games in six days and regularly led the majors in innings pitched. He won a league-leading 31 games for the Giants in 1903, 35 in 1904, and, with Mathewson, formed a one-two punch that would not be equaled until Sandy Koufax and Don Drysdale teamed up for the Dodgers in the 1960s. McGinnity retired from the majors in 1908, at age 38, but kept pitching in minor league and semi-pro games until he was 54.

Iron Man McGinnity twice won over 30 games and often pitched both ends of a doubleheader.

31

A chorus line of six
Giants before a 1912
game: *left to right,*
Rube Marquard,
Charles Tesreau,
Christy Mathewson,
Leon Ames, George
Wiltse, and Jim
Crandall.

Official Score Card
New York Giants vs. Boston Red Sox
Champions of the National League   *Champions of the American League.*

Our Record
Year — Position
1903 —
1904 — 2nd.
1905 — 1st.
1906 — 2nd.
1907 — 4th.
1908 — 2nd.
1909 — 3rd.
1910 — 2nd.
1911 — 1st.
1912 — 1st.

At the
BRUSH
STADIUM

WORLD'S
CHAMPIONSHIP
SERIES · 1912 ·

John T. Brush Pres.

Price
10 Cents   Harry M. Stevens Publisher

A program from the ill-fated 1912 World Series, which the Giants lost to Boston in eight games (including a tie game called for darkness).

Dummy Taylor, the comic deaf-mute, spent eight years with the Giants, posting an impressive 114-103 record and winning 21 games in 1904. He was heckled by crowds at first, but after he started to win, and after the Giants learned sign language, he became a favorite, bringing fans to their feet when he would hold up three fingers to announce he would strike out a batter with two strikes already on him.

"Turkey" Mike Donlin was another gifted player, a good-looking, hard-living star who fell in love with and married Mable Hite, a nightclub and stage super-

star. Donlin hit over .300 in three of his four full seasons with the Giants, but he left after the 1908 season to form a vaudeville act with his young wife, who died soon after of cancer. After a fling in Hollywood, appearing in several Buster Keaton films, he returned to pinch hit for the 1914 Giants.

Another slugger, and Hall-of-Famer, was George "Highpockets" Kelly, who got his nickname because he wore his pants' pockets set high. For six years in a row in the 1920s he batted over .300 for the Giants and once hit seven home runs in six games.

The team had its outcasts, too, like Bugs Raymond, a promising pitcher and a hopeless drunk. Unable to stay sober for long, he had an erratic career with his finest season being his 18-12 year for McGraw in 1909. McGraw's repeated efforts to reform Raymond failed, and the pitcher died after being beaten in a barroom brawl at age 30.

But all of their feats pale in comparison to those of the great Christy Mathewson, the best pitcher of his time—perhaps the best of any time. In his 17-year-long career (all but the last season and a half spent with the Giants), Matty won 373 games, the most by any National Leaguer, reigned as national checkers champion for years, and posted 30-win seasons three

33

CHRISTY MATHEWSON

Christy Mathewson was president of his class at Bucknell, the star of its football team, and, as an afterthought, the best pitcher in the world. His achievements as a hurler with the Giants at the turn of the century are more dazzling than any of the pulp-fiction magazines about ballplayers that sold so well at the time. And on the side, he was the national checkers champion many years running—before baseball games he would play checkers against six people at a time.

But these things alone could not have made the great Matty the legend that he was. The pitcher came up at the turn of the century, when baseball was struggling to get a toehold. Most ballplayers were rough around the edges, playing dirty and fighting constantly. The dashing, good-looking Mathewson, with his college degree and college manners, helped draw millions of women and children into ballparks, changing the look of the game forever.

Above, cardboard fans like this one with Mathewson's smiling face on it were handed out at the ballpark on hot summer days.

Right, Mathewson, like everybody else, made money on the side hawking products. On this cardboard broadside he's pitching Tuxedo cigarettes.

Pitching in a Pinch was one of several books the popular Mathewson wrote with a ghostwriter. The title came from his oft-quoted threat that in tight games he always held something back in case he had "to pitch in a pinch."

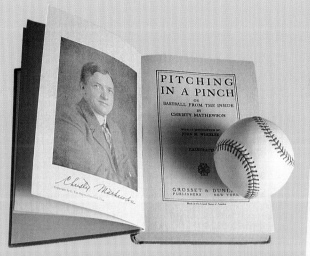

Mathewson, New York Nationals

St. Nicholas was a boys' magazine from the Thirties that always published baseball covers during the season; this issue also carried a story about Mathewson, the cover boy, still a legend five years after his death.

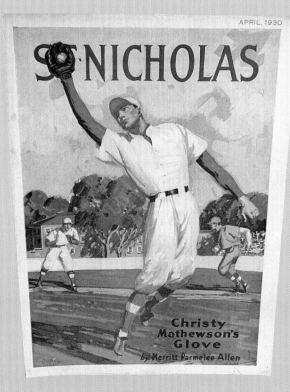

APRIL, 1930

ST. NICHOLAS

Christy Mathewson's Glove
by Merritt Parmelee Allen

Few photos captured the heroic appearance of pitcher Christy Mathewson like this 1908 Piedmont tobacco card. Manufacturers slid one card into each pack of tobacco; kids who collected them had a lot of explaining to do to their parents.

Above, one of the few remaining booklets chronicling the Giants' 1913 world tour, the first such trip taken by a baseball team since 1889.

Above, John McGraw shakes hands with Ben Franklin on the cover of this 1913 World Series program. It wouldn't be long before Muggsy would be sick of Franklin and Philadelphia: the A's beat his Giants in the Series of 1911 and 1913.

A press pin from the 1913 Series.

years in a row. His finest year came in 1908 when he won 37 games. Nicknamed "Big Six" after the big New York fire engines of the era, Mathewson was one of only three pitchers in history to master the screwball (the Giants' Carl Hubbell and the Dodgers' Fernando Valenzuela were the others). Besides being a pitching genius, he was college educated, courteous, a snappy dresser, and was single-handedly responsible for the tremendous surge of women and children who started coming to baseball games after 1903.

Matty was a kind-hearted soul, too. When he was well ahead in a game, he would walk off the mound and ask an opposing player which of his teammates needed hits to bring up his average. The player would give him the names of two or

Christy Mathewson on the mound.

McGraw won his third straight pennant with his well-stocked 1913 team, shown here from a 1914 program. The club featured three pitchers who won 20 or more games: Mathewson, spitballer Jeff Tesreau, and Rube Marquard. Chief Myers, one of several Native Americans playing major league ball at that time, hit .312. If you look closely you'll see the best athlete of the era, Jim Thorpe (*back row, fourth from right*).

three batters in deep slumps. "Tell them to hit the third pitch," Matty would say. Then, good as his word, he'd let each slumping batter get one or two hits, and the game would end 11-4 instead of 11-0.

And finally, of course, there was Charles "Victory" Faust, a spectator dressed in a black suit who introduced himself to McGraw in St. Louis at the start of the 1911 season. Faust told the manager that a fortune teller had predicted he would pitch for the New York Giants and lead them to a pennant. McGraw gave him a tryout. Faust was pathetic. So McGraw signed him as a macabre good luck charm, paying him out of his own pocket. As luck would have it, as soon as Faust joined the team the Giants went on a winning streak,

the streak became plural, and the team won the pennant that year.

McGraw had Faust warm up before and during every game, but he never put him in. The good luck charm would sit on the bench spouting out predictions like "Giants win next three in a row," and the team would promptly win three straight. Or he'd say, "Giants 7, Pittsburgh 4," and the next day the Giants would beat Pittsburgh 7-4. It was uncanny.

Faust begged McGraw to put him on the mound, but the manager kept refusing. Finally, in the ninth inning of the last game of the season, with the pennant wrapped up and the Giants leading, 5-2, McGraw put Faust in against last-place Brooklyn. The crowd went wild. The Brooklyn players,

Left, this rare 1917 Giants versus White Sox program is one of the finest in existence. The following year, major league baseball would play a shortened schedule with mostly minor leaguers on the field as the nation was plunged into World War I.

Right, a press ribbon from the 1917 World Series.

happy to be part of the gag, deliberately struck out or hit easy infield grounders so that Faust could quickly retire the side. McGraw then juggled his lineup so Faust could come to the plate. The Brooklyn pitcher hit him, lightly and quite deliberately, to get him on base. McGraw then ordered Faust to steal second, and the catcher, holding his throw a moment, let him do it. Then Faust stole third and finally home as the crowd cheered.

It was this galaxy of characters and talent that McGraw harnessed to make the Giants the dominant team of the period, winning ten pennants between 1904 and 1924—including three straight from 1911 to 1913, and four straight from 1921 to 1924—and taking the World Series in 1905, 1921, and 1922.

They won and lost with style, too, and in bizarre fashion. For the 1905 World Series with Philadelphia, as a psychological ploy McGraw had his team dress in menacing black uniforms. The Giants, looking like a dugout full of Darth Vaders, took the championship. They tried the same black uniform in 1911 but they lost.

The team always seemed to be involved in legendary plays, too, like the Merkle boner. Another memorable moment came in the final inning of the

A 1914 Cracker Jack card featuring Matty in his last days with the Giants.

McGraw's autograph dwarfed everyone's, as did his presence on the field or in a room. This 1925 ball was also signed by Frankie Frisch, the "Fordham Flash."

Although this looks like a strange bat, actually it is a New York cop's 1920s billy club, used to break up riots, and carried by police at the Polo Grounds.

final game of the 1912 World Series against the Red Sox when center fielder Fred Snodgrass dropped an easy fly ball, one any Little Leaguer could catch, enabling Boston to win, 3-2.

There were several factors that made the Giants the focus of baseball in the first quarter of the century, the glamour team in what was rapidly becoming a glamour game. One was New York City, itself. Dramatic increases in population due to immigration during the 1880s had made big American cities bigger, and none had grown like New York. In 1898 Brooklyn and its 1.4 million residents had become part of New York as well, doubling the size of the city. As New York grew, so too did its influence. Theodore Roosevelt, a New Yorker, served as president at the time McGraw began winning pennants for the Giants. During the first quarter of the century the American theater flourished, the

Rube Marquard was a star pitcher for both the Dodgers and the Giants, the latter from 1908 to 1915.

movie industry sprang up, and the stock market burgeoned—all in New York.

So the Giants found themselves representing the biggest, brawniest city in the nation. It amplified everything the Giants did.

When the Roaring Twenties began, however, John McGraw was irritable and angry. His pennant-winning team of 1917 had fallen apart. Even though they'd only slipped to second place in 1918 and 1919, for the high-riding Giants of those days second seemed like last. But what irritated McGraw more than his second-place finishes was another local team called the Yankees. Since 1913 the Giants had permitted the Yankees to play their home games at the Polo Grounds and the Yankees had repaid them by outdrawing them at the box office and out-inking them in the newspapers. In short, they were becoming the new darlings of the city. And what really irked McGraw about the Yankees was Babe Ruth. Made an outfielder so he could play every day, the Bambino had become the superstar of the game, crashing an unbelievable 54 home runs in 1920. The following year he was knocking down walls again on his way to a miraculous 59 homers. Everybody in town was talking about Ruth, not about the Giants.

McGraw was upbeat about some

Frankie Frisch, the "Fordham Flash," practices one of his patented head-first slides. Frisch was a member of the Giants' 1924 infield, every player on which made the Hall of Fame.

Commemorative medals like this were common in the Twenties.

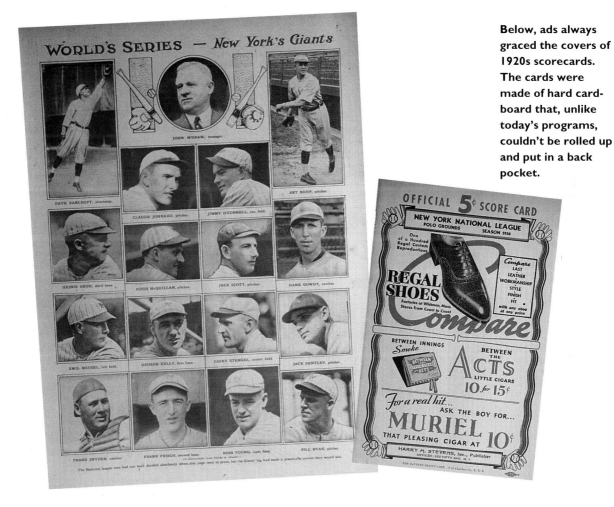

WORLD'S SERIES — New York's Giants

JOHN McGRAW, manager

DAVE BANCROFT, shortstop.

CLAUDE JONNARD, pitcher.   JIMMY O'CONNELL, cen. field.   ART NEHF, pitcher.

HEINIE GROH, third base.   HUGH McQUILLAN, pitcher.   JACK SCOTT, pitcher.   HANK GOWDY, catcher.

EMIL MEUSEL, left field.   GEORGE KELLY, first base.   CASEY STENGEL, center field.   JACK BENTLEY, pitcher.

FRANK SNYDER, catcher.   FRANK FRISCH, second base.   ROSS YOUNG, right field.   BILL RYAN, pitcher.

Below, ads always graced the covers of 1920s scorecards. The cards were made of hard cardboard that, unlike today's programs, couldn't be rolled up and put in a back pocket.

Above, this rare, glossy page from the *New York Times* of the 1922 Giants has become a collector's item. Except for Heinie Groh, each of the starting fielders hit .327 or higher.

things, though. For one, the team had new owners. After Brush died in 1912, his son-in-law Harry Hempstead had taken over and things went on pretty much the same. But in 1919 a syndicate headed by Charles Stoneham purchased the Giants and gave Muggsy McGraw part ownership. McGraw was also confident that his 1921 roster

was one of the best Giants teams ever. He had strong returning players like Highpockets Kelly, Frankie Frisch (the Fordham Flash), Ross Youngs, Larry Doyle, and pitchers Fred Toney, Art Nehf, and Jesse Barnes. He made trades that brought on board Casey Stengel, Dave Bancroft, Johnny Rawlings, and Irish Meusel.

Nonetheless, the team was sluggish and stumbled through the early part of the season. Mathewson had retired—he was suffering from tuberculosis as a result of the gas poisoning he sustained in World War I — and throughout the season McGraw would telephone the ailing Matty to give him an inning-by-inning, blow-by-blow account of each game. As the gap between the first-place Pittsburgh Pirates and the second-place Giants grew, so did McGraw's rage. Finally, unable to take it anymore, he called a team meeting before the start of an August home series against the Pirates, who were then leading by 7½ games. What followed, players said, was a tongue-lashing that would have put Knute Rockne to shame. Calling them bush league players (in saltier language), McGraw declared that the Giants weren't capable of beating Pittsburgh or anyone

A Giants pennant from the mid-1920s.

else—and that he would no longer have anything to do with them. Then he turned his back on the team and walked out. The next day, game one of the series, he wouldn't speak to anyone. He stood in a corner of the dugout, arms crossed, eyes frozen on the field, and for two hours said not one word. The chastised and inflamed Giants beat the Pirates, 10-2, took the second game as well, swept the series, and, fighting hard all the way, went on to win the pennant by four games. Only to face . . . the Yankees.

The 1921 World Series was a publicity bonanza for both clubs. It was the very first New York–versus–New York championship contest. Writers dubbed it the Subway Series because fans of both clubs could get to the Polo Grounds (home to both clubs) on the trains. McGraw howled when his club, which owned the stadium,

Discussing ground rules before the first game of the World Series, October 5, 1921. The Giants are represented by coach Dave Bancroft, far right.

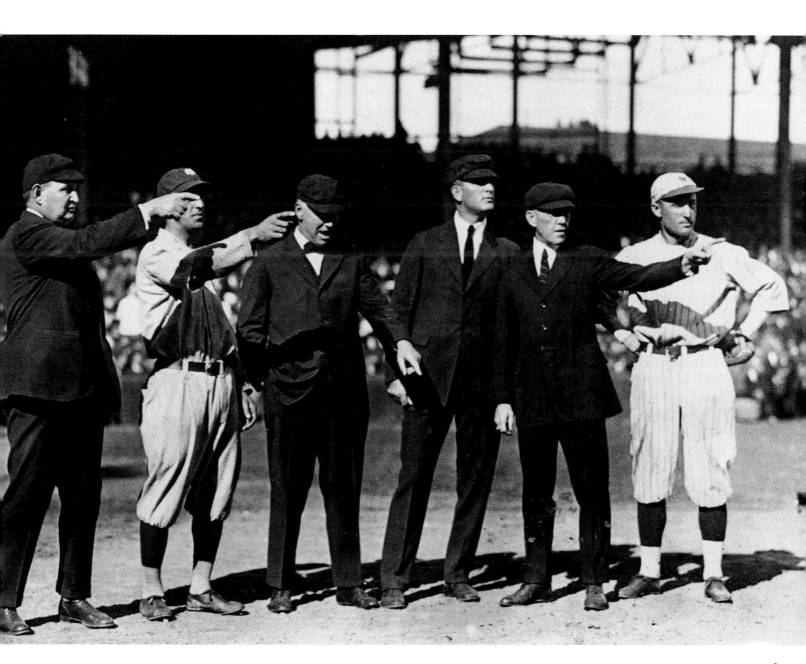

45

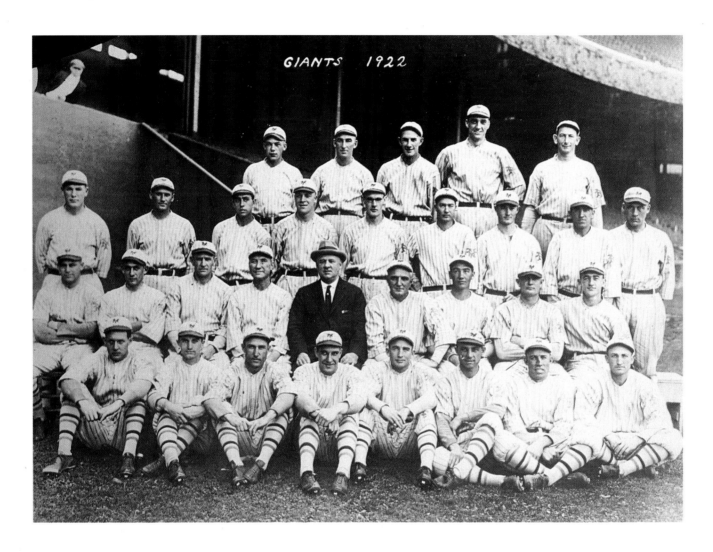

GIANTS 1922

The Giants of 1922 were one of the most powerful teams ever to play baseball, registering a team batting average of .304 (with .368 for Stengel). They won the pennant handily that year and crushed the Yankees in a five-game series, holding the mighty Babe Ruth to a .118 average.

This historic ball is from the final play in the game that wasn't—the oddest moment in the 1922 World Series. The ball was caught by the Giants' first baseman to end the tenth inning of a tied game two. But right after the putout the umpire mysteriously called the game on account of darkness, even though the sun was still shining. The game was ruled a tie.

was ordered by the commissioner of baseball to wear road jerseys for half the games because someone had to be the visitor. The papers went wild speculating what Ruth would do to Giants pitching. "Don't throw that big baboon anything but low curves," McGraw ordered his pitchers.

The Yanks won the first two games and the Giants the next two, with Shufflin' Phil Douglas the winning pitcher in game four. (He served up the only home run the great Ruth would get in the series.) Game five, as you might expect with the Giants, was unusual. When Ruth came swaggering to the plate in the fourth inning the Giants'

infield and outfield moved back. But the Babe stunned the crowd by laying down a perfect bunt and beating the throw to first. A much faster runner than people realize, he then made it home on a Bob Meusel double. It was a costly dash for the Giants, who ended up losing, 3-1, but even more costly for the Yankees—Ruth collapsed in the dugout and manager Miller Huggins announced the slugger was through for the Series.

With Ruth on the bench, the Giants evened the Series in game six and pulled ahead in game seven (teams had to win five games then). Game eight was an odd one too. The Giants took a 1-0 lead into the ninth when, in a moment of sheer drama, Huggins sent Ruth to the plate as a pinch hitter. The crowd roared, but Ruth grounded out. Then the Yanks' Aaron Ward walked, bringing up Home Run Baker. Baker hit a rope between first and second. Rawlings dove at it and somehow managed to knock it down. He picked it up as he was rolling over, got to his knees, and threw Baker out at first. First baseman Kelly, his eye on Ward sprinting toward third, fired the ball to Frisch, who tagged Ward out as he slid. The Giants won the world championship for the first time since 1905.

Right after the season, still full of bravado, McGraw kicked the Yankees out of the Polo Grounds. If this was war, he

47

The second Polo Grounds at Coogan's Bluff, built in 1912 and home to many of baseball's great moments.

felt, the Yanks were going to have to build their own bunker. The result was the hurried construction of Yankee Stadium, which opened in April 1923.

For 1922 McGraw wanted an even stronger team than his 1921 world champions, and Stoneham was eager to please

him. The Giants signed Heinie Groh, a third baseman; shortstop Travis Jackson, who would go into the Hall of Fame; and, best of all, Hall of Fame first baseman Bill Terry, a wunderkind hitter who would bat .401 in 1930 and go on to manage the Giants from 1932 to 1941.

Below, a sportswriter's 1925 season pass.

Above, this decorative jersey was worn in 1925 to celebrate the fiftieth anniversary of the National League.

Pulling off another championship wasn't easy. There was enormous pressure from fans and writers for the Giants to repeat and for the Yankees to meet them again in the World Series. The season was full of tension and at first the Giants weren't handling it very well. By mid-July the vaunted pitching staff was stumbling. Terry was still being groomed in Toledo (he wouldn't come up till late in the 1923 season). Several players had drinking problems and certain others took it upon themselves to personally close all the nightclubs and kiss all the girls in Manhattan. Then, in mid-August, Shufflin'

Phil Douglas was kicked out of baseball permanently for writing a letter to a St. Louis player suggesting that, for a fee, he would sit out the rest of the season, thus giving the Cardinals a shot at the pennant.

The Giants' cream finally rose to the top, though, and the team won the pennant. And, just as New Yorkers had wished, they once again met the Yankees and Ruth at the Polo Grounds for a second Subway Series. Perhaps stronger than at any time in their history, the Giants shelled the Yankees, four games to none, holding the mighty Ruth to a .118 series batting average.

49

A medal commemorating the Giants' 1929 season.

As it turned out, the most memorable event of this series was an umpire's call in game two. The match proceeded slowly and moved into extra innings with the score tied, 3-3. The tenth inning ended at 4:45 P.M. with the sun still high in a blue sky. Suddenly umpire George Hildebrand called the game—on account of darkness. A near riot ensued.

The Giants won pennants again in 1923 and 1924 and finished second in 1925, 1928, and 1931. But they would never win another World Series under McGraw and the team would slip toward the end of the Twenties. McGraw did all he

could, even trading for National League MVP Rogers Hornsby, but the slugger from St. Louis wound up being more trouble than he was worth. Nothing seemed to work for the Giants. Finally in the middle of the 1932 season, a disgusted McGraw turned the team over to first baseman Bill Terry. Although no one knew it then, no National League manager would ever head a team for that long again (29 consecutive seasons). No man would ever win pennants in three different decades again. And no one team would ever dominate the National League over the course of three decades again. McGraw had been a giant.

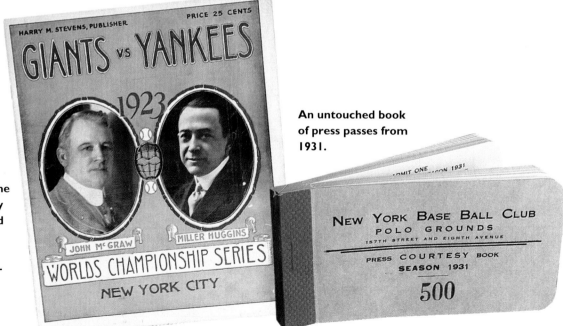

A program from one of the early Subway Series, which pitted the Giants against the Yanks in 1923. Behind Ruth's powerful slugging, the Yanks prevailed in seven games.

An untouched book of press passes from 1931.

Bundled up against the October chill, an unidentified Giant heads for home during the 1924 World Series against the Washington Senators. The Senators won the Series in the seventh game with a 12-inning heartbreaker.

MEMPHIS BILL, KING CARL, & THE NEW AGE
1932–1956

Bill Terry looked like a movie star with his swept-back black hair and handsome face. Tall and wide-shouldered, he looked great in a suit and could have easily passed for a matinee idol or a business mogul. But it was in a jersey, not a suit, that Terry became legend. Known as "Memphis Bill," he did not arrive in the majors until he was 26 years old. He'd been in and out of baseball, at one point even beginning a career as a junior executive with the Standard Oil Company. After a season in Toledo in 1922, Terry was picked up by the Giants and worked his way into the lineup at first base. He would become one of baseball's top hitters. He flowered in 1925, batting .319, and went on to hit over .350 in four different seasons. In 1930 he finished the season at .401, the last National Leaguer to hit .400. Over his 14-season playing career, he compiled an impressive .341 average.

What was most remarkable about Memphis Bill, though, was that he was able to keep hitting when McGraw asked him to take over as the club's manager in 1932. Up to then. baseball had seen many player-managers, but few good ones. The job of running the club never diminished Terry's ability to power the club. He kept right on hitting over .300 for the next four years, giving up playing after a .310 1936 season to manage full-time.

Generations of Giants convened at the Polo Grounds when manager Bill Terry greeted Jim Mutrie, the team's first manager from back in 1884.

Right, lots of teams barnstormed in the Thirties. This 1936 broadside advertises the dream pitching matchup between

18-year-old rookie sensation Bob Feller and King of the Hill Hubbell during a barnstorming tour.

BASEBALL

NEW YORK GIANTS VS. CLEVELAND INDIANS
(National Champions)

Auspices of The American Legion and Columbia Senators

Wouldn't you like to see BOB FELLER, the 18 year old "Rookie Wonder", pitted against CARL HUBBELL, "The Southpaw Ace"

Carl Hubbell, "The Southpaw Ace" *Bob Feller, "The Rookie Wonder"*

PARTIAL ROSTER

NEW YORK		CLEVELAND	
Bill Terry	Melvin Ott	Steve O'Nell	Joseph Heving
Carl Hubbell	Henry Leiber	Hal Trosky	Earl Whitehill
Gus Mancuso	Burgess Whitehead	Bob Feller	Tom Drake
Richard Bartell	John McCarthy	John Allen	Adell Hale
Louis Chiozza	Harold Schumacher	Bruce Campbell	Lyn Lary
Joe Moore	Harry Gumbert	Mell Harder	Earl Averill

Dreyfuss Field, Thursday, April 15
3:00 P. M.

...sion: Bleachers, tax included, 60c; Grandstand, tax included, $1.20

Above, an extraordinary art deco cover appearing on the 1933 World Series program.

Above, this marvelously preserved Giants ball was signed by Carl Hubbell, Mel Ott, and Ernie Lombardi, among others.

Terry, who never got along with the press, did an extraordinary job as manager. After he inherited the team in mid-season, he turned the sixth-place club of 1932 into the pennant winners and world champions of 1933, then went on to win two more pennants in the next four seasons. Terry's style was decidedly different from McGraw's. Muggsy was an aggressive, bombs-away manager who won big games with big bats. Terry was a conservative, defensive manag-

Bill Terry at bat. He was the last National Leaguer to hit over .400 when he averaged .401 in 1930.

er who relished one-run wins. In fact, during his first five years he had only two dependable bats in his lineup—his own and Mel Ott's (the latter dubbed by the press Mellifluous Melvin or Master Melvin).

Terry's style worked, but it didn't hurt that he had the best pitching staff in all of baseball. The team's meal ticket was Carl Hubbell, the screwball wizard. He was joined by Roy Parmalee, Freddy Fitzsimmons, and Hal Schumacher, and the four together were an awesome collection. In 1933 Hubbell won 23 games, Schumacher 19, and Fitzsimmons 16; in 1934 it was Schumacher 23, Hubbell 21, and Fitzsimmons 18; in 1935, Hubbell 23, Schumacher 19, and Parmalee 14.

Hubbell was the engine. One of the most remarkable pitchers of all time, King Carl absolutely baffled batters with his windmill windup and screwball. He posted a career record of 253 wins and 154 losses, including five consecutive 20-game seasons, and was named MVP twice. Hubbell did everything, including relief, and in 1934 he registered eight saves. At the end of the 1936 season he won 16 games in a row—a

**"Prince Hal"
Schumacher, a
mound ace for the
Giants in the 1930s.**

streak he continued over the first eight
games of the 1937 season for an
unmatched streak of 24. He once hurled
an 18-inning six-hitter, winning 1-0. But
he'll be remembered most for his performance in the 1934 All-Star Game when he
struck out five consecutive Hall-of-
Famers—Babe Ruth, Lou Gehrig, Jimmie
Foxx, Al Simmons, and Joe Cronin.

"I was up that second inning, and of
course I struck out, too," remembered
Lefty Gomez, the opposing pitcher. "I
watched it all close up and I'll tell you, and
I'm telling you this as a pitcher, nobody,
and I mean nobody, ever pitched that well
for two innings. Hell, in my dreams I never
pitched that well."

Hubbell's arm and the bats of Ott and
Terry took the Giants to the 1933 World
Series against the Washington Senators.
The Giants beat the Senators the same
way they beat everybody else—careful
play, a few explosive bats, and Hubbell.
King Carl won game four, 2-1, with a stel-
lar 11-inning performance. Game five, the
Series clincher, was won on a tenth-inning
home run by Ott. It was the Giants' first
world championship in a decade and the
celebrating ran long into the night.

The team played well again in 1934,
but a late-season slump left them two
games behind the pennant-winning

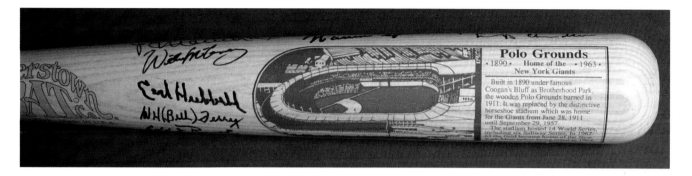

In 1987, the Cooperstown Bat Company began producing stadium bats like this Polo Grounds model. Fans then went out and got players to sign them. Carl Hubbell and Bill Terry, who both lived to ripe old ages, inked this one.

A 1932 newspaper drawing of Len Koenecke pasted into an old scrapbook. Koenecke's was a strange fate. After playing the 1932 season for the Giants he was traded. But on a plane home after he was let go in 1935, the reportedly drunk Koenecke got into an argument with the pilot and in the ensuing brawl he was killed.

Left, the 1933 National League champions, preserved forever on the pages of a fan's scrapbook.

The Washington Senators' Joe Cronin dives back to first to avoid a pickoff in the third game of the 1933 World Series, which the Giants ultimately won.

King Carl Hubbell in the locker room after the 1934 All-Star Game, in which he struck out Babe Ruth, Lou Gehrig, Jimmy Foxx, Al Simmons, and Joe Cronin—in a row.

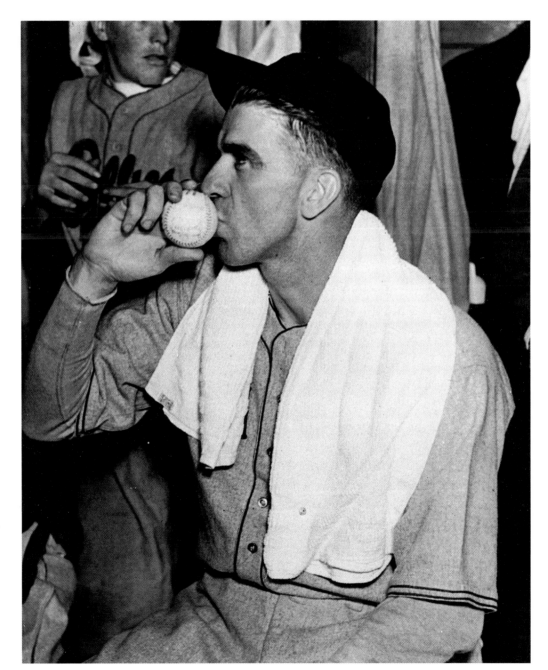

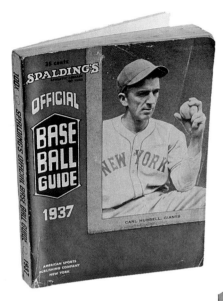

Who else but **Carl Hubbell** would be on the cover of the '37 *Spalding Guide* after his memorable 26-6 season the year before?

Cardinals. They finished third in 1935, but jumped right back into first in 1936, winning the flag by five games, aided by the infield play of shortstop Dick Bartell. That year they met the Yankees in the first Subway Series since 1923. With Hubbell on the mound, the Giants won the opener, 6-1, but the Yankee bats came alive in game two—every man in the lineup had at least one hit—and smashed the Giants, 18-4. The Yanks, with stars like Lou Gehrig,

Carl Hubbell (*second row, third from left*) anchored the 1937 Giants, which won the pennant by three games. They were stopped for the second year in a row in the World Series, though, this time going down in just five games to the Yanks. This newspaper page was saved by a New Jersey collector who put it in his scrapbook when he was eight years old.

N. Y. GIANTS — NATIONAL LEAGUE CHAMPIONS—1937

Front row: Burgess Whitehead, 2b.; Joe Moore, l. f.; Frank Snyder, coach; Manager Bill Terry; Dolf Luque, coach; Gus Mancuso, c.; Sam Leslie, 1b.; Don Brennan, p. Second row: Hank Leiber, c. f.; Tom Baker, p.; Carl Hubbell, p.; Cliff Melton, p.; Dick Coffman, p.; Harry Gumbert, p.; Johnny McCarthy, 1b.; Wally Berger, o. f.; Bloody Ryan, inf. Back row: Harry Danning, c.; Hal Schumacher, p.; Jimmy Ripple, r. f.; Mel Ott, 3b.; Al Smith, p.; Ed Madjeski, c.; Dick Bartell, ss., and Lou Chiozza, c. f.

An ambitious fan got all the 1936 Giants pictured here to sign this team roster. Coach Adolfo Luque (*top right*) had been one of the Cuban stars to move to the majors in the early 1920s.

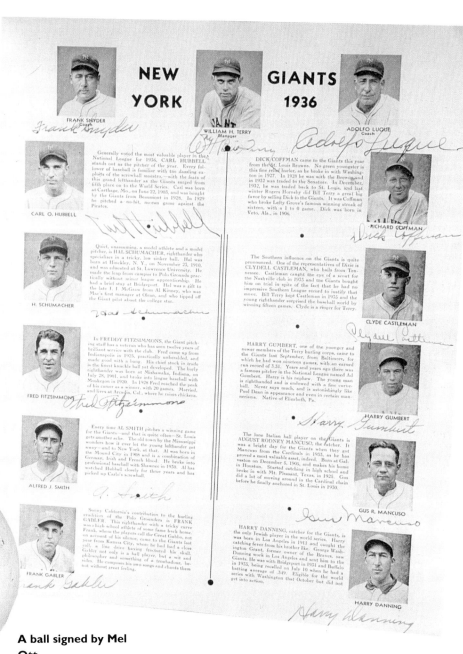

A ball signed by Mel Ott.

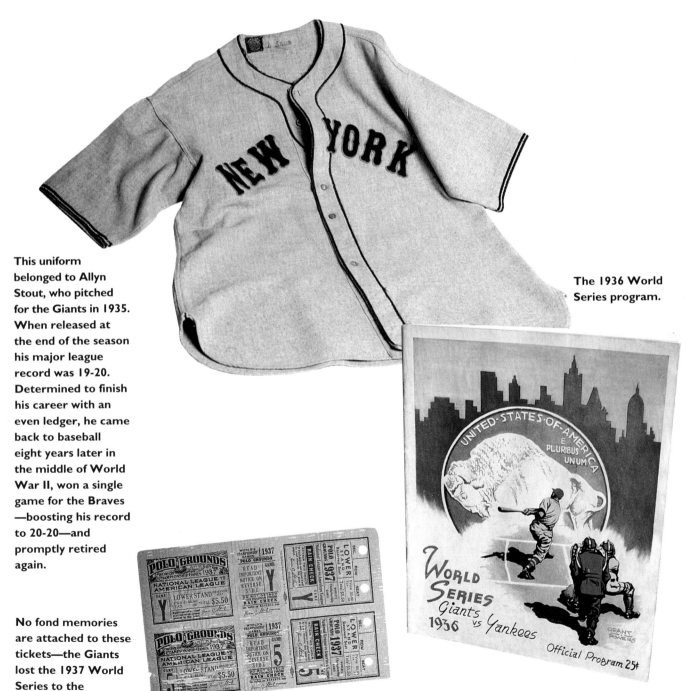

This uniform belonged to Allyn Stout, who pitched for the Giants in 1935. When released at the end of the season his major league record was 19-20. Determined to finish his career with an even ledger, he came back to baseball eight years later in the middle of World War II, won a single game for the Braves —boosting his record to 20-20—and promptly retired again.

No fond memories are attached to these tickets—the Giants lost the 1937 World Series to the Yankees.

The 1936 World Series program.

Carl Hubbell warms up before the 1937 World Series.

Bill Dickey, Lefty Gomez, Red Ruffing, and hot rookie Joe DiMaggio, went on to take the Series four games to two—the first of the four straight world championships that started their 30-year domination of the American League.

Undaunted, Terry's Giants repeated as National League champs in 1937, the year Hubbell stunned baseball with his winning streak. But again they were no match for the Bronx Bombers, who won the World Series in five games.

Those mid- and late 1930s Giant teams were nearly always in the first division and big fan favorites. Travis Jackson, a Hall-of-Famer with a long and consistent career, played third base. Gus Mancuso, a dependable catcher who hit .301 in 1936, handled the pitchers. Outfielder Jo Jo Moore hit .310 in 1937, when the Giants repeated as pennant winners. The next year, when the Giants slipped to third, catcher Harry Danning hit .306, followed by .316 the next year.

But the lynchpin of the offense in just about every year of the late Thirties and early Forties was Mel Ott. Mellifluous Melvin hit .311 lifetime with 511 home runs and 1,860 RBIs. He led the league in homers six times and made ten consecutive All-Star teams. And he accomplished all that with his bizarre foot-in-the-bucket swing. The lefty would raise his right foot

Home run king Mel Ott, who hit 511 out of the park, takes his fabled foot-in-the-bucket stance.

as the ball came in, step forward to whip his body into the ball, and then step out and down, still swinging. The results were tremendous.

"When he started hitting all those home runs everybody tried to do it, but nobody could. We couldn't play trumpet like Louis Armstrong, either," said Ted "Double Duty" Radcliff, a Negro Leaguer who competed against Ott frequently in exhibition games.

Ott couldn't do the job alone, however. Following the back-to-back pennants in 1936 and 1937, the Giants slid into a long slump, finishing near the bottom of the division in 1939, 1940, and 1941. The next year the Giants acquired help in the form of Johnny Mize, the beefy slugger from St. Louis. Dubbed "the Big Cat" by Stan Musial, he hit 26 homers before leaving the team for the service. After the war, he became the most feared slugger in the National League.

The war years were fallow ones for the Giants. Like everyone else, they filled their roster with teenagers and old men, minor leaguers and college boys. Mize, Harry Danning, Babe Young, and Willard Marshall left to fight. Some players, including Mel Ott, remained. Ott was made manager in 1942 and, like his predecessor, he continued to play. But he couldn't do much with

Above, the signa-
tures of Mel Ott and
other Giants grace
the balls on left and
right, but the sweet
spot on the center
ball is covered with
the signature of E. T.
"Glass Arm" Brown,
a Giants player who
made it to majors at
the age of 31 and was
best known for his
arm's inability to
reach much of any-
thing.

Rogers Hornsby,
who played for the
Giants in the late
1920s, signed the bat
on top, while Babe
Ruth, Mel Ott, and
others signed the
bottom one.

65

The "Big Cat," Johnny Mize, connects.

Everybody loved the Giants in New York. I played just about as many years for the Cards and the Yankees, but nobody remembers that. When people meet me they say, "Oh, Johnny Mize, of the Giants." There was always something about the Giants that people connected to.

—JOHNNY MIZE, Giants

66

Harry "the Horse"
Danning, the Giants
catcher in the
Thirties.

MEMPHIS BILL, KING CARL & THE NEW AGE

A 1941 Giants program from the Polo Grounds, signed by Jocko Conlan. A fan spotted the retired umpire, a Hall-of-Famer, at a baseball card show and remembered that Conlan had umped the game in this program, so Conlan signed the cover. "A great ballpark," he told the fan, "They'll never make 'em like that again." Next to it is a souvenir straw hat sold the first year the Giants were in San Francisco.

Right, Horace Stoneham, the Giants owner who would get more headlines for abandoning New York than winning championships in it, is depicted here in this program with his front office.

A hat worn by one of the Giants players in the 1940s.

the team and by mid-1943 they were in last place. Ott as manager was like Ott as player—one of the nicest people in baseball (which prompted Leo Durocher's immortal line about the likeable Ott and his team: "Nice guys finish last.").

During the war the Giants held victory rallies in the Polo Grounds, dressed in red, white, and blue game uniforms, sold

Mel Ott, he of the foot-in-the-bucket stance, was quickly dubbed "Mellifluous Melvin" by sports-writers. Here he's on the cover of the *New York Daily News* magazine in 1942.

Johnny Mize, who crashed 359 career homers, with Ralph Kiner, who whacked 369, on an issue of *Who's Who in Baseball*, 1948.

war bonds, and trained close to home, at the Rockefeller estate in Lakewood, New Jersey. Like everyone else, they respected the president's curfew, calling games one hour after sundown so that Nazi bombers couldn't use the ballpark lights to help target the city (really).

As dreary as the Giants were in the early Forties, they got worse when the war ended. The team finished fifth in 1944 and 1945, and slumped to last in 1946, the year that most of the roster went south—to the rogue Mexican League. That year two Mexican teams decided that what they needed to boost attendance was a strong infusion of American stars. An equal opportunity employer, first they raided the Negro Leagues and landed several of their superstars, including Ray Dandridge and Monte Irvin, the latter of whom won the Mexican Triple Crown in 1941. Then they turned their sights on the majors and signed stars like home-run king Vern Stephens. Other teams suffered loses— Max Lanier of the Cardinals went, and Dodgers catcher Mickey Owen—but none as bad as the Giants, who lost six players to the siren song of pesos and finished at the bottom of the league. As it turned out, most of the major leaguers left Mexico after their first year. Kept out a season by the commissioner, they eventually returned to their teams.

69

Ike won the war and a day for himself at the Polo Grounds. These stubs and the program are from the Giants' salute to Eisenhower in 1945.

What really annoyed the Giants fans in the summer of 1946, however, was the Dodgers. While their boys were floundering in the cellar of the National League, the hated Dodgers were skimming along, their skipper Leo Durocher keeping them ahead of just about everyone. Then, in 1947, the baseball world was stunned when the commissioner of baseball accused Durocher of associating with gamblers and suspended him for the season. The Giants fans, who hated Leo the Lip, were delighted. Durocher returned to his post in 1948, but midway through the season the Dodgers fell into last place and the manager was let go. Then, in one of the great turnarounds in sports, Horace Stoneham signed Durocher to manage the Giants. Giants fans never really grew to love Leo, but they were sure happy about what he did.

Durocher inherited a sluggish ball club and at first he couldn't do much with it. The team finished fifth in both 1948 and 1949. Then he convinced Stoneham to spend some money and make some trades. By 1950 the Lip had Don Mueller, Wes Westrum, Bobby Thomson, Whitey Lockman, Al Dark, Monte Irvin, and Eddie Stanky in the field, with Sal Maglie and Larry Jansen on the mound. The Giants finished a very respectable third.

This souvenir patch was sold at the Polo Grounds in the late Forties.

The *New York Daily News* went to spring training in 1949 to snap these pictures of the Giants.

The next year looked to be a good one and everyone at the Polo Grounds knew it. Sure, the Yankees were loaded again, and so were the Dodgers—oh, were they loaded. But Durocher's Giants had everybody back from the previous year, along with an unknown kid who'd learned his baseball as a teenager in the Negro Leagues—Willie Mays. When the Giants called him up from the minors he was hitting .477. Read it again, four seventy-seven. But he came to New York and fell flat on his face, going 0-for-12 in his first four games. Finally, four games into his major-league career, he broke through the slump, smashing a Warren Spahn curve up and out of the Polo Grounds—not just out of the playing field but out of the ballpark altogether. Mays went on to hit .274 that year, and belted 20 home runs—the first

71

A signed ball and a pin, artifacts from Mays's brilliant career.

Stamp books like this one, bought by kids in the Fifties, are today considered some of the finest memorabilia of the era. The Giants book was one in a series.

of a career total of 660 that placed him third on the all-time list. But it was more than his bat and his electrifying catches that changed the Giants (he later admitted that he always wore a cap one size too small so it would fly off on a run). With his happy-go-lucky style and cheery clubhouse attitude, Mays had a way with fans and fellow players that made him an instant hero. The "Say Hey" kid played stickball in the streets of Harlem with youngsters and chatted with everyone. Mays gave the Giants an important spark.

But even with Mays's presence, the Giants seemed pretty much finished by early August. They were 13½ games behind the Dodgers, who were getting

ready for another World Series shot against a Yankee powerhouse that included Joe DiMaggio and rookie outfielder Mickey Mantle. Then, in the middle of August, Leo started to work his magic, taking his players aside—at the Polo Grounds, in opponents' parks, on train cars—urging them to do better, always encouraging them, never chastising them. Little by little, the Giants started to do better, to win more, slowly to close the gap on the Dodgers.

Monte Irvin, his shoulders still broad and his arms still muscular at age 67, smiles easily when he remembers that season. Now assistant to the commissioner of baseball, he is the same elegant, impeccably dressed gentleman he was in 1951.

Dave Koslo, Monte
Irvin, and Al Dark
celebrate their first
game win over the
Yankees in the 1951
World Series.

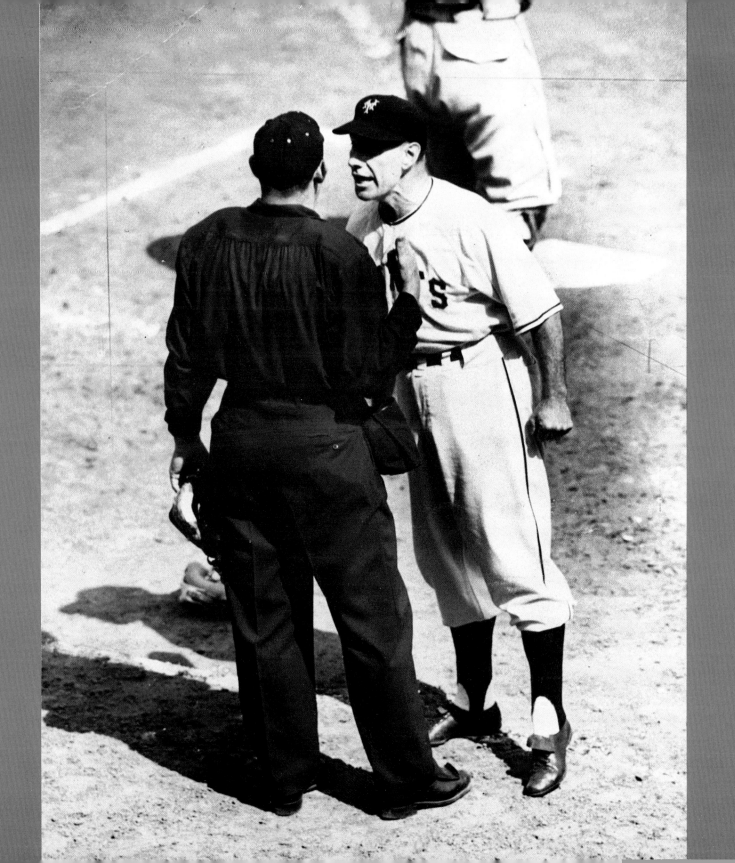

Manager Leo Durocher in his most familiar pose, arguing with an umpire.

One of Monte Irvin's signed bats. The slugger played eight record-breaking seasons in the Negro Leagues before he—along with Larry Doby, Willie Mays, Jackie Robinson, and others—helped break the color line in the majors.

"Leo Durocher was the greatest manager of the era. He knew how to motivate people by what he said and, more importantly, by what he didn't say," explained Irvin. "When we were 13½ games back of the Dodgers that year, he never tried to drive us to catch up. It was never 'We've got to sweep the Cardinals!' It was always 'Come on now, let's take two out of three.' Even at the end when we were pulling within a game or two, he'd urge us to 'play a little better, try to win some games.' So we were never in a panic or in a sprint. We just played hard and tried to win each day. I don't think, being so far back, that we could have done it if the manager did push us."

Everybody knows the story, so it needs little retelling. You can be brief about how Moses led the Israelites out of Egypt, too. On the final day of the season, the Giants caught the Dodgers, tying them for first. The commissioner called for a best-of-three playoff for the pennant, a subway playoff as intense as any Subway Series. "Remember now, that this wasn't

like the Red Sox–Yankee playoff in '78 where the teams went back and forth between cities hundreds of miles apart," pointed out Duke Snider. "We were a couple of train stops apart, that's all, so in each game, at each ballpark, half the crowd was yours. It was loud, let me tell you." The Dodgers won one, the Giants won one, and the teams jumped on the subway for game three at the Polo Grounds—a game that was destined to live forever in sports history.

It isn't possible to describe what happened at the Polo Grounds in the third playoff game without setting the stage. The Dodgers and the Giants were fierce and historic rivals meeting in the rubber game of the playoff. The winner would directly to the World Series against the third New York team, the hated Yankees. The Giants had come an incredible distance, all the way from 13½ games back, to get to this moment. The Dodgers were fielding one of their strongest teams ever. Fans from both sides jammed the Polo Grounds for the afternoon game. The tension grew

THE SHOT HEARD 'ROUND THE WORLD

I didn't think home run. I just wanted to hit it fair some place.

—BOBBY THOMSON, former Giant

The dotted line shows the path of Bobby Thomson's historic home run that won the third and final game of the National League playoffs in 1951.

One of many balls Bobby Thomson has signed since his historic home run in the 1951 playoffs.

Bobby Thomson, who hit the ball, and Ralph Branca, who threw it, both signed this edition of *The Miracle of Coogan's Bluff*, about the miracle finish of 1951.

I t [the Bobby Thomson home run] is all people have talked to me about for these 42 years and all they talk to me about today. At first I didn't mind, but then after about ten years of it I got pretty fed up. For the next 20 years I hated to talk about it. Then in the early '80s I stopped caring.

I was a good pitcher, 88-68, and in 1947 I won 21 games, but all anybody will remember me for is Bobby's home run. I could have amassed ten fortunes and discovered a planet, but I know that when I die, the first line in all the obituaries the next day will say, "Ralph Branca, the man who threw the home run to Bobby Thomson. . . ."

—RALPH BRANCA, Brooklyn Dodgers

Bobby Thomson's jacket.

Press credentials for the 1951 World Series.

with each inning. Finally, with one out in the bottom of the ninth, it looked like the end for the Giants, who were trailing Brooklyn, 4-2. They had two men on when Yankee pitcher Don Newcomb, who was tiring fast, asked manager Charlie Dressen to take him out. Dressen obliged and brought in relief pitcher Ralph Branca, wearing number 13 on his back, to face the Giants' Bobby Thomson. With Willie Mays in the on-deck circle, everyone in the ballpark rose to their feet.

Russ Hodges, working the game for WMCA radio, called the next play:

Bobby Thomson up there swinging. . . . He's had two out of three, a single and a double, and Billy Cox is playing right on the third base line. . . . One out, last of the ninth. . . Branca pitches and Bobby takes a strike call on the inside corner. . . Bobby hitting at .292. . . . He's had a single and a double and drove in the Giants' first run with a long fly to center. . . . Brooklyn leads it, 4-2. . . . Hartung down the line at third, not taking any chances. . . . Lockman without too big a lead at second, but he'll be running like the wind if Thomson hits one. . . . Branca throws. . . . There's a long drive. . . . It's gonna be. . . . I believe. . . . THE GIANTS WIN THE PENNANT! THE GIANTS WIN THE PENNANT! BOBBY THOMSON HITS INTO THE LOWER DECK OF THE LEFT FIELD STANDS! THE GIANTS WIN THE PENNANT AND THEY'RE GOING CRAZY!

World Series tickets from 1951.

Durocher reads the story of the world champion 1951 Giants to one of his players on this 1952 program cover, but the team did not repeat, finishing four and a half games behind the cross-town Dodgers.

Players surrounding the downed Monte Irvin, who broke his leg sliding into third in an exhibition game prior to the 1952 season and was lost for the year.

The fans started to pour onto the field as Thomson rounded the bases. His teammates smothered him. He leaped high in the air and then down into the middle of a crowd of players and onto home plate. Thousands more swarmed onto the field. An hour later, the field still covered with fans, Thomson emerged onto the short porch of the clubhouse in center and waved to the fans, who went crazy all over again.

The next day the papers put the game in proper perspective with other events in the universe. "The Miracle of

Press club cards of the celebrated AP sports writer Joe Reichler, who would later create the venerable *Encyclopedia of Baseball*, the fan's bible.

No. 57
POLO GROUNDS PRESS CLUB
Membership Card
1955

No. 69
POLO GROUNDS PRESS CLUB
Membership Card
Joe Reichler (Associated Press
1954

No. 70
POLO GROUNDS PRESS CLUB
Membership Card
1952
Committee

Below, the Giants barnstormed through Japan in 1953. Here's a ticket stub from one of their games—in Japanese.

Giants
日米親善
内野席券 ¥400
場所・後楽園球場
期日 10 月 19 日
主催・読売新聞
非課税
昭 28年10月分証
1953
3
本券は雨天其の他の都合により四回半を終了せる場合は予備日又は順延日に有効文京
開催日時は読売新聞紙上に発表いたします。

Coogan's Bluff!" blared one. "Shot Heard 'Round the World" screamed another. And so it was.

The Giants, perhaps winded by their sprint to the pennant playoff and the three-game Armageddon with the Dodgers, lost the 1951 World Series to the Yankees in six games, one a 13-1 rout. The following spring, Monte Irvin broke his leg and was carried off the field on a stretcher before a horrified Polo Grounds crowd. A month later Willie Mays left the team and went into the army. Without Irvin or Willie and his famous basket catches, the Giants slipped a bit, finishing 4½ games behind the Dodgers. In 1953, still without Willie, they collapsed, finishing 35 games back. Not only did they get battered, they got ugly. During a September 6 game with the first-place Dodgers, a full-scale melee broke out between the two teams, still smoldering over an altercation two days before. No one is sure who started it, but before it was over, the brawl had escalated into one of the scariest incidents in baseball history and one that fanned the flames of the ongoing Dodgers-Giants feud.

Another historic—and portentous—event that year was the Braves' move out of Boston and into the new Midwestern market, in their case to Milwaukee. The

81

Below, this Giants souvenir cup is illustrated with the Polo Grounds.

Opposite, in what the experts regard as the greatest catch of all time, Willie Mays, after a long sprint, hauls in Vic Wertz's towering drive to deep center in the first game of the 1954 World Series. The underdog Giants went on to win, four games to none.

Above, an ambitious fan ran down to the rail in the 1954 World Series and had both skippers, the Giants' Durocher and the Indians' Al Lopez, sign this program.

Below, a 1954 World Championship ring.

team owners had complained bitterly for years that they could not turn a profit in a small stadium in a city with two teams. The success of the Braves' move, the first by a National League team in half a century, was watched closely by Giants owner Stoneham and Dodgers boss Walter O'Malley.

In 1954, everything turned around for the New York team. Irvin was 100 percent, the Say Hey kid was back, and the loaded Giants played hard from wire to wire, taking the National League pennant by five games and steaming into the World Series. They were huge underdogs. The

American League champs, the Cleveland Indians, had stunned all of baseball that year by winning 111 games and dumping the Yankees.

But before the first game was over, the underdogs had turned into top dogs. Willie Mays's memorable over-the-shoulder catch of Vic Wertz's 440-foot fly ball set the tone for the entire series, marking the Giants, not the Indians, as the team to beat.

Just about every baseball fan has seen film footage of Mays's electrifying catch, his spinning turn, hat flying, and his throw to second. Everyone is startled by it—everyone but Willie. Looking back on the play

WILLIE MAYS

I never cared about the records. I never counted my home runs in August. I never figured out my batting average. None of that mattered. All that mattered was that I was out there playing baseball and that people liked to see me play.

—WILLIE MAYS, Giants

Right, Mays's 1960 jersey, with his signature below the "4."

Willie finished his career where he started it—in New York—but with the Mets, not the Giants. On behalf of the city that loved him through 22 years of baseball, Mayor John Lindsay gave him this silver bowl as a token of Gotham's appreciation.

There has always been this big controversy about who was the best center fielder in New York in the Fifties—Willie, Mickey, or the Duke. I always avoided the issue, but I'll tell you, it was Willie. If you're going to compare anybody in baseball you've got to use the numbers. Look at Willie's numbers—660 homers, the 1903 RBIs, the .302 average. He did it all against the best in the business. He never sat down—played 20 some years. Who was the best? It was Willie.

—MICKEY MANTLE, New York Yankees

WILLIE MAYS
FROM THE CITY OF NEW YORK
MAYOR
SEPTEMBER

This collage frames Mays's career and includes an unusual 33 rpm record on the life and times of Willie.

These Giants Polo Grounds programs include the very last one, from 1957.

years later, Mays still doesn't think it was that good. "I got a real good jump on it, saw the arc of the ball, and got up a lot of speed. I knew I'd catch it. I knew I'd be there. Hey, I didn't even dive for it. I've certainly made better catches than that."

New York's 5-2 victory in the game shook up the Indians, who never recovered. The Giants took game two, 3-1, behind pitcher Johnny Antonelli, who'd had a super 21-7 season that year. They took game three, 6-2, with Ruben Gomez on the mound. The sweep was completed in Cleveland with a 7-4 win in game four.

But the euphoria of a world championship, the Giants' first in 21 years, didn't last long. The team stumbled through the next spring and summer, finishing in third place, 18½ games back of the Dodgers, who went on, at last, to win a World Series themselves. The Giants' front office, reeling more than the fans, reacted swiftly, firing Durocher, but it did little good. The new manager, Bill Rigney, promptly led the Giants to a sixth-place finish in both 1956 and 1957 as attendance plunged.

Meanwhile during 1956 and 1957, under a lid of secrecy, Dodgers owner O'Malley courted the city of Los Angeles. Hearing of his meetings with the mayor of Los Angeles, San Francisco's mayor, George Christopher, went to see O'Malley, who went to see Horace

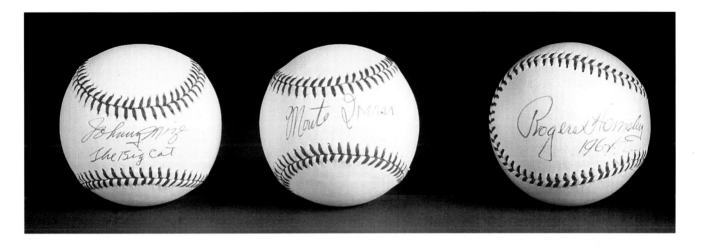

Balls signed by
Johnny Mize, Monte
Irvin, and Rogers
Hornsby.

T he Giant teams of the early Fifties were
among the best in baseball—ever. Look at
the '51 team, the heart it had, coming from
13 games back to win the pennant. The '54 team
was a tremendous ballclub. Everybody was
shocked when we swept the Indians in the Series.
I wasn't.

—LEO DUROCHER, Giants manager

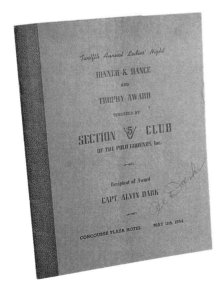

Shortstop Al Dark
signed this 1954
awards banquet pro-
gram, held after the
team won the World
Series that year.

87

Giants owner Horace Stoneham *(third from left)* listens to Dodgers general manager Walter O'Malley *(far left)* as he tries to convince a solemn New York mayor Robert Wagner and others to help the two teams stay in New York. A year later, in 1958, they were gone.

Stoneham, who went to see Christopher. By the summer of 1957 both the Giants and the Dodgers had agreed to flee New York and relocate on the West Coast. Baseball was surprised. New York was shell-shocked.

It was unthinkable. Two of the greatest franchises in baseball history had pulled out of the nation's number one population and media market at the same time, leaving New York with only the Yankees, and

Dodger and Giant fans with absolutely nothing.

Fans were livid. "When we learned the Giants were leaving town we were crushed, just crushed," remembered fan Larry DeRosa, who had gone to the Polo Grounds to watch the Giants for nearly 40 years. "They dumped us, abandoned us, and for what? For money, that's what. We supported them all of our lives. They were there for, what, 80 years? Generations of

A copy of the Giants' 1955 schedule, inserted in the *New York Daily News* for all the local teams in its Sunday papers each spring.

my family went to the Polo Grounds to support the Giants. Generations. Then they left. One day we had this great baseball team and the next day we had nothing. I couldn't continue to be a Giants fan after they left. I couldn't even get the awful words 'San Francisco' out of my mouth. So, like many others, I just forgot about the Giants. I became a Mets fan. I still am."

But in 1957, who could imagine a team called the Mets? Their beloved Giants were gone, and New Yorkers were deep in mourning.

A bobbin' head doll stands guard over this old scoreboard number a fan retrieved the day they tore down the Polo Grounds.

CHAPTER FOUR

HELL GATE TO GOLDEN GATE

The Late Fifties and Sixties

The Giants could not have moved farther from home than to San Francisco, the alabaster city on the Bay, the town Tony Bennett left his heart in, where Sam Spade chased the Maltese Falcon and grizzled gold miners had gone to play. The Golden Gate was a long way from Hell Gate, the Grand Concourse, FDR Drive, the East River, Coogan's Bluff, and all the other locales the Giants had thrived in for 75 years in New York.

Most Californians welcomed the Giants with open arms. San Francisco had made a name for itself in sports with its football 49ers, Kezar Stadium, a popular minor league baseball club called the Seals, and Bill Russell's teams at the University of San Francisco. Lefty O'Doul, the great slugger, was a native, and both he and Joe DiMaggio, who hailed from the area, had played for the Seals. Yet there was a hole in the heart of the city.

"In 1957, most San Franciscans still did not see their city as a big-league town," explained long-time fan Ed Weinberg. "They still felt, as people in Los Angeles felt, that they were stepsisters in sports. We were separated by half a country from all the baseball. They felt a big-league baseball team would make San Francisco a big-league city. And it did."

When the Giants arrived, the mayor threw parties for them, politicians and civic leaders honored them, fans bought season tickets,

The newly arrived Giants, swapping one coast for another, are treated to a boisterous parade in downtown San Francisco.

The old and the new.

The Congress of Racial Equality gave Willie its Lifetime Achievement Award.

and kids sought their autographs. But not everyone was enamored with the Giants.

"I think a lot of people held back from supporting the Giants for two reasons," said Dick Dobbins, an ardent Giants fan who was himself a skeptic in 1958. "First, the Seals had left town, bought by the Red Sox. The Seals and minor league baseball were institutions here. People loved them. They saw the arrival of the Giants as the reason the Seals left. It wasn't true, but people saw it that way. Second, this was not *our* team. This was New York's team. We inherited it, had it mailed to us, dropped on our doorstep. It wasn't a whole new team, like the Astros and Mets were four years later."

The doubters were a minority, though. The Giants had so many new fans on the shores of the Pacific that Seals Stadium was packed whenever they were in town. In 1958, their first West Coast season, they drew 1.3 million fans and 1.44 million the following year. In 1959, in fact, they drew more fans than they would in 17 of their first 30 years at Candlestick Park, the windy new stadium they built in 1960, and they did it in an old 22,000-seat park.

An aerial view of
Candlestick Park.

Willie Mays's 1962 Giants jersey and one of the signed gloves he used that year. Once the great fielder dropped four fly balls in a single day, after which he took out a knife and cut his glove into a thousand pieces. Asked if maybe it wasn't the glove's fault, Mays answered gravely, "I don't drop fly balls."

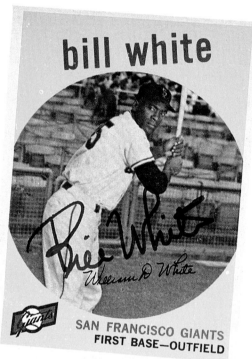

First baseman Bill White starred for the San Francisco Giants and later became president of the National League.

've been a Giants fan all my life, and I mean all of it. We moved to San Francisco when I was age 16 months. It was '61. My father was a crazy Giants fan. He used to go see them at the Polo Grounds when he lived in New York. I always secretly thought he got a job out here to follow the Giants west.

—ED CRESPE, 32, of Modesto

The Giants made a number of shrewd moves. A few years back, perhaps looking down the road, they'd picked a Bay Area native, Bill Rigney, as New York manager. Now in 1958 they hired Jerry Donovan, president of the Seals, as an executive. They openly courted Seals fans as well as supporters of San Francisco's many other pro and college teams.

"It wasn't sophisticated marketing, not like in the late 1970s, but it worked," admitted Arthur Schultz, the Giants' ticket manager, who came to San Francisco with the club. "I think many people in San Francisco wanted a major league team very badly. I mean, look at the attendance at tiny Seals Stadium, some 16,000 a game. That alone shows how hungry people in the area were for major league baseball and the Giants."

Many of the mainstays of the New York Giants were gone—Bobby Thomson, Don Mueller, Dusty Rhodes, Wes Westrum, Hank Thompson. Willie Mays was there but he was unhappy, for as it turned out, San Francisco, like most other places, had its bigots. Willie and his wife found they couldn't move into the neighborhood they wanted because they were black. Later, someone tossed a brick through their living room window. And Willie got little support at the ballpark. He was New York's superstar, not San Francisco's, and he'd trot out onto the field to icy stares and scattered boos. To make matters worse, manager Bill Rigney charged up expectations to unrealistic levels by announcing Mays was certain to hit 61 home runs in Seals Stadium.

The Giants had finished an atrocious 26 games back in 1957, but they had a lot of young talent in their inaugural season in the Bay Area. There were new outfielders all over the place—Felipe Alou, Willie Kirkland, Jackie Brandt, and Leon Wagner. Bill White was back from the Army. The pitching looked good, too, with Johnny Antonelli, Mike McCormick, and Ruben Gomez returning to the mound.

Mays as represented by two figurines and a popular Sixties bobbin' head doll.

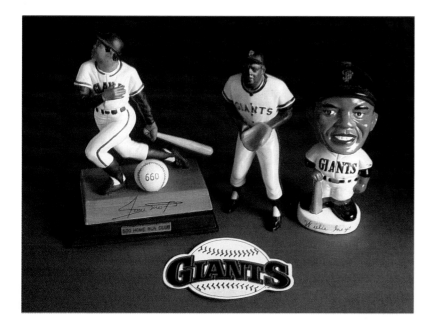

The "Baby Bull,"
Orlando Cepeda.

96

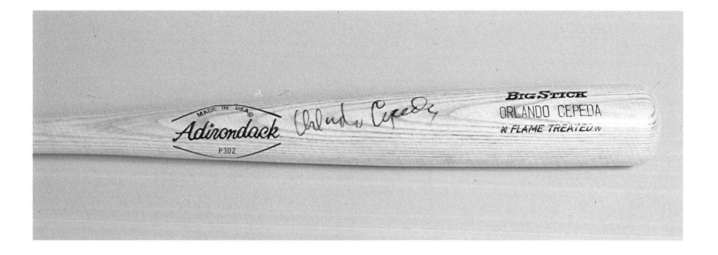

Orlando Cepeda signed this bat.

And best of all there was Orlando Cepeda, the outrageously talented and powerful rookie first baseman. The six-foot, two-inch 210-pound slugger from Puerto Rico ripped a titanic home run in the Giants' very first home game at Seals Stadium, a shot that immediately endeared the rookie, *their* rookie, to the California fans. That year the "Baby Bull" won Rookie of the Year honors with 25 home runs, 96 RBIs, a league-leading 38 doubles, and a .312 batting average. He went on to have a long run of memorable years in San Francisco before he was injured and then traded to St. Louis in the mid-1960s. In 1959 he hit .317 with 105 RBIs. In 1961 he smashed 46 home runs and had 142 RBIs, leading the league in both stats. In 1962 he batted .306 with 35 homers. The next year

he hit .316 and .304 in 1964, the year he was named to his sixth straight All-Star team. The fans loved him because he was talented and good with kids. But best of all, Cepeda was their own new superstar, not one of those second-hand imports from New York. When the fans voted for the team's Most Valuable Player in 1958, it was Cepeda, not Mays, who got the honor.

Mays, too, had a great year in 1958, with 29 home runs and a .347 batting average, followed up in 1959 with 34 homers and a .313 average. The Giants stayed close most of that first year, but finished 12 games behind the first-place Braves. In 1959, with Mays and Cepeda returning, the club started to put together a new team, a franchise team with San Francisco as its true home and players who had no tales to

97

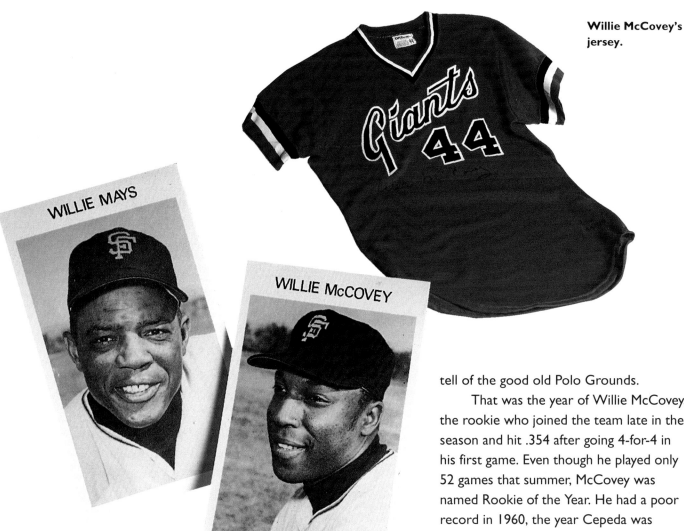

Willie McCovey's jersey.

WILLIE MAYS

WILLIE McCOVEY

Between them, Willie Mays and Willie McCovey smashed an incredible 1,121 home runs, an average of one per game for nearly ten years.

tell of the good old Polo Grounds.

That was the year of Willie McCovey, the rookie who joined the team late in the season and hit .354 after going 4-for-4 in his first game. Even though he played only 52 games that summer, McCovey was named Rookie of the Year. He had a poor record in 1960, the year Cepeda was moved from first to the outfield to make room for Willie, but he bounced back in 1961 and 1962. In 1963 his 44 home runs put him on top of the National League along with Hank Aaron. His 1968 and 1969 figures of 36 and 45 were league-leaders as well. A prodigious home run hitter, he was

always near the top in the majors and finished his career with a total of 521 for a
tenth-place tie with Ted Williams in the all-
time major league rankings.

The team began to jell in 1960 with
Mays, McCovey, and Cepeda at the heart
of the batting order. Near the midpoint of
the season the Giants were sizzling with a
33-22 record. Then suddenly Bill Rigney
was fired following a sweep by powerful
Pittsburgh. Tom Sheehan was appointed
interim manager and the team stumbled to
a fifth-place finish.

Alvin Dark, a no-nonsense player
who became a no-nonsense manager, was
named the new skipper, and players and
fans realized right away that this was a new

ballclub. Dark did not hobnob with writers
the way Rigney had, or Durocher before
him. He wanted his own operation, too,
and in spring training he released Lefty
O'Doul, the San Francisco hero and spring
training volunteer batting coach whom
fans venerated. Dark stuck up for his players and entered dozens of fierce disputes
with umpires in order to back up their
plays. Within weeks the new manager had
built a new spirit on the team. The Giants
did better in 1961, finishing up in third
place, eight games out of first.

By opening day, 1962, the San
Francisco Giants featured a majority of
players who had joined the team since it
moved West. There were a few holdovers,

**McCovey signed this
model bat for a fan
and added** *San
Francisco Giants* **to it.**

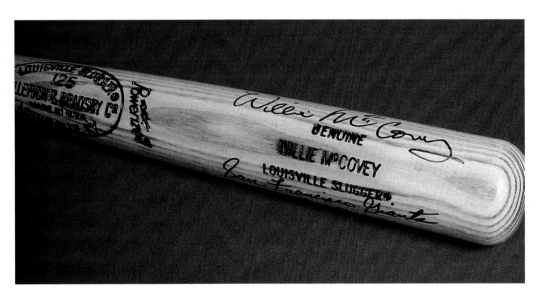

99

To show their support for the new ballclub, San Franciscans line up outside just-completed Candlestick Park a week before the stadium's April 12, 1960, opener.

like Mays and pitcher Stu Miller, but not many. New players were everywhere, from hitters like Cepeda, McCovey, and Jim Davenport to pitchers like Jack Sanford and the fabulous Juan Marichal.

"I think in that time, four years, the team had changed to 'our' team," recalled fan and Giants memorabilia collector Duane Garrett. "Around that time, '61 to '62, the fans changed. It wasn't an imported club anymore. It wasn't a New York club anymore. It was now, finally, a totally San Francisco club and, from, the fans' view, 'ours'—at last. From '62 on, the San Francisco Giants were truly the San Franciscans' Giants."

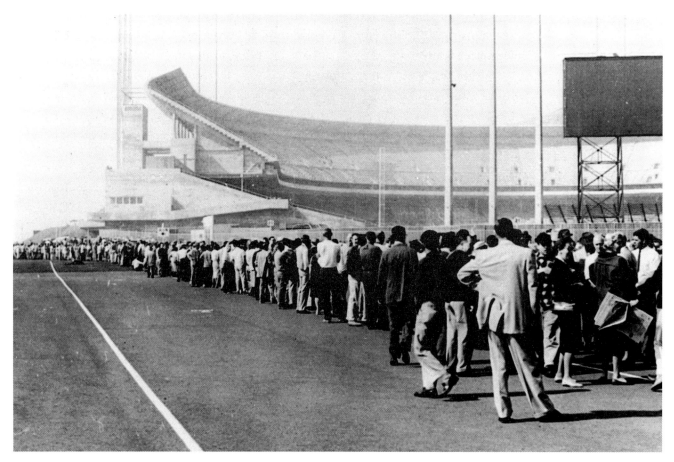

Mays was one of the premier cover boys of the Sixties.

Nineteen sixty-two was also the year that the Giants and Dodgers really renewed the spirited rivalry they had carried with them from New York, where it had been the hottest in the history of baseball. With 387 miles between the two teams instead of the Brooklyn Bridge, the intensity would never be as torrid as it had been, but the Dodgers versus the Giants in California have always made sparks fly.

"The rivalry is big in California in a different way," explained Duke Snider, the former Dodgers star and now a broadcaster. "In New York, the two teams and boroughs were right on top of each other, and sure, it was stronger, especially when Leo jumped from the Dodgers to the Giants. But here in California there are a lot of other factors we didn't have in New York. I think San Francisco and L.A. are always competing with each other to be California's number one city, and not just athletically. They compete fiercely in the business, cultural, and political worlds. The baseball teams have come to symbolize that terrific rivalry between the two cities."

Families, friends, and even roommates split down the middle on the Dodgers-versus-Giants question. Rosa Huerta is a big, big Giants fan and a big, big Dodgers hater. "I'm not one of those people who say, 'I hate the Dodgers.' I really do hate the Dodgers," she insisted. "I think they are overrated as ballplayers. They play dirty. Their pitchers, back through Drysdale, have always thrown at people's heads in order to win. I also can't stand anything about Los Angeles. I think it's an overrated town and I think the people

CANDLESTICK PARK

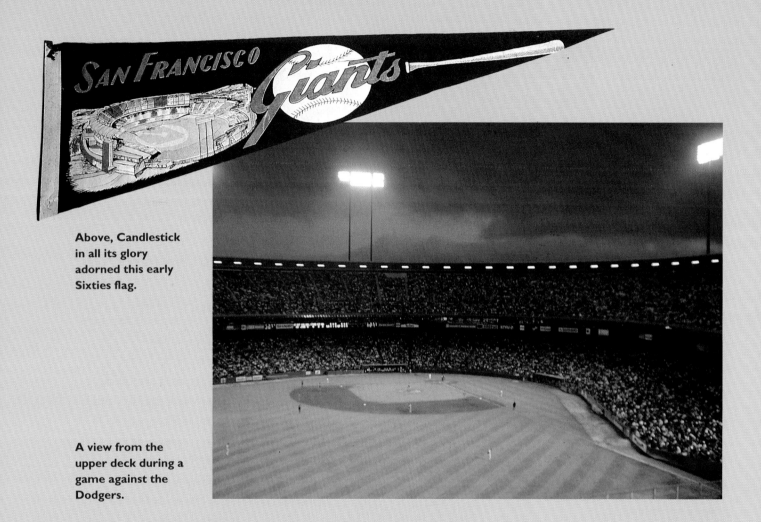

Above, Candlestick in all its glory adorned this early Sixties flag.

A view from the upper deck during a game against the Dodgers.

The Giants began looking for a site for their stadium as soon as Horace Stoneham made up his mind to take the team to San Francisco. The site the club finally chose was at Candlestick Point, which jutted out into San Francisco Bay from the southeast corner of the peninsula. People from the Seals, whose stadium they used in the interim, warned the

Giants about building a ballpark at Candlestick. The point was constantly whipped by swirling winds from the Pacific and the Bay, and temperatures plunged precipitously at night. Others warned the club that there was no public transportation to Candlestick and that the only road serving the area was Highway 101, already overcrowded with commuter traffic.

But no one listened and Candlestick Park opened on April 12, 1960. The park originally seated 42,500 for baseball (62,000 since 1989).

To help the stadium and the franchise get on its feet, Major League Baseball decided to hold its annual All-Star Game at Candlestick in 1961. The event highlighted the ballpark's problems in memorable fashion: the winds coming in from the Bay over the open outfield fence were so strong they actually blew pitcher Stu Miller off the mound.

The turbulent wind has been a problem ever since, as has the weather. "Day games are fine, but you must wear a sweatshirt, and maybe a sweatshirt plus jacket, on a summer night, which is crazy," said souvenir vendor Steve York of Richmond, bundled up in his own Giants jacket. "The wind will often blow trees halfway over. You feel like you're in a hurricane for nine innings on some nights."

Players have trouble in the park when the wind acts up. Pop-ups in the infield become high drama. "Ordinarily a fielder calls for a ball, waits, and catches it. Here, the entire infield starts to maneuver on a pop-up because you don't know where it will come down," said Dodgers shortstop Dave Anderson. "As it does come down, the guy who's going

This framed and festooned photo of Candlestick in 1991 captures the park in all its glory.

CANDLESTICK PARK

One of the most sought-after San Francisco souvenirs is this ticket stub to the first game ever held at Candlestick; the yellow circle is a dressing room press pass from 1962.

to catch it has to whirl about in circles to follow it as the wind takes it back and forth. You look like one of those guys in the circus balancing a pole."

The owner agrees with everyone. "Looking back, the team should never, ever have built this stadium," admitted Bob Lurie. "It was just a bad idea from the beginning and we're stuck with it."

Despite all of that, the Giants have thrived in Candlestick. It has hosted the 1961 All-Star Game, the 1962 playoffs, the 1971 playoffs, the 1987 playoffs, and the 1989 World Series. And it has survived a major earthquake in style.

"For all its faults, history will always remember it as the place where Willie Mays played center field, and that is enough," said former Giant Brett Butler.

Willie Mays at bat for the new San Francisco Giants.

who live there are sissies. And I think they are very jealous of the nice people who live in San Francisco and wish they had a great baseball team like the Giants."

Vicki Gonzalez, on the other hand, is a rabid Dodgers fan and hates the Giants. "The Dodgers have style and grace. The Giants always look like they're ready to fall down," she explained. "The Dodgers

emphasize teamwork. The players on the Giants are all out for personal glory. There's no question the Dodgers are a better baseball team. Besides, when we get into a World Series, we win them, unlike the Giants, who always lose them."

Someone should keep these two apart, right? Guess again—they're room-mates. They share an apartment in San

105

Willie McCovey springs toward first in the 1962 World Series, the first at Candlestick; Willie failed to beat out the throw and the Giants failed to beat the Yanks in the Series.

106

Francisco. Can you just imagine the arguments when the Dodgers play the Giants on television? "Oh, no," smiled Rosa, nudging her roomie with her elbow. "When they play each other on TV what we do, by mutual agreement, is never watch. That way we stay roommates."

The Dodgers-versus-Giants question splits families, too. Mike Flynn lives in Sacramento, a 90-minute drive from Candlestick Park. He loves the Giants dearly and he always takes his ten-year-old son, Jeff, with him to Giants games. The problem is that Jeff is a diehard Dodgers fan who absolutely hates the Giants. Even

If there was anything Mays was more famous for than the home run it was the basket catch. This is his 1962 Golden Glove award, given annually to the best fielder.

at home Mike has no respite. When the Dodgers and Giants are on different television channels at the same time, it is always the Dodgers games the family watches. "Sure, and the reason is that my wife, who's supposed to be the objective arbiter, is a Dodgers fan, too." complained Flynn. "In many ways, democracy stinks."

There was no question that, except possibly for the Dodgers, the Giants were the best team in the National League in 1962. And there was no question that, except possibly for the Giants, the Dodgers were the best team. At the end of the season, still no one could tell which was better. The Giants had started slowly but finished strong, powered by Willie Mays, who led the majors with 49 home runs. They got a tremendous performance from pitcher Jack Sanford, who won 24 games—including 16 in a row to tie the one-season record Hubbell had set in 1936. On top of that Billy O'Dell won 19 and Juan Marichal 18.

But the Dodgers were hot, too. Maury Wills startled pitchers, catchers, and fans from coast to coast by stealing 104 bases, breaking Ty Cobb's 1915 mark. Tommy Davis hit .346, and Don Drysdale picked up a Cy Young Award with his 25 wins. But the Dodgers were haunted by a mid-July injury to star pitcher Sandy

ON WILLIE McCOVEY

A great, great baseball player, a man who never gave up.
> —Former Giants owner **BOB LURIE**

An all-around player, able to do anything for you. He always got the clutch hit, always drove in the important run.
> —**WILLIE MAYS**, Giants

He hit everybody and he hit everywhere. Didn't matter what park he was in or whether he was home or away. He killed everybody.
> —Giants coach **DUSTY BAKER**

McCovey's jacket.

Willie McCovey homers against the Braves.

A Giant is safe at home on this mid-Sixties pennant.

Koufax, who lost all circulation in his fingers and was benched for the rest of the year. As soon as he left the rotation, the Dodgers' slump began. They lost again and again and, at the end, dropped ten of their last 13 games.

Still, on the last day of the season, even as they were losing their last game, the Dodgers remained in first. But the Giants pulled up to tie them, beating the Astros on a Mays home run. "That was one of my best moments," said Mays. "It was a home run that really counted."

A three-game playoff series began at Candlestick Park with the injured Koufax back on the mound for Los Angeles. The Giants, still hot, plastered Koufax, 8-0, with the Say Hey kid hitting two home runs. The playoffs then moved to the

Dodgers' brand new stadium in L.A., where the home team won the second game. But the Giants came back to win game three by scoring four runs in the ninth. They had their first pennant in eight years, and—at the expense of the hated Dodgers—it was a specially delicious one.

Looking back, the 1962 Giants were one of baseball's all-time best teams. Four pitchers won 16 games or more. Cepeda hit .306 with 35 homers. Mays hit .304 along with his 49 homers. McCovey, playing little more than half the season, hit 20 homers. Jim Davenport hit .297. Felipe Alou hit 25 homers and averaged .316. Even Harvey Kuenn, in his twilight years, hit .304. This team had heart, too, never giving up while the Dodgers were running away with the league.

The Giants celebrate
their final-game
victory over the
Dodgers in 1962, a
triumph that gave
them their first pen-
nant in eight years.

Above, another heartbreak for the Giants came in 1965 when they finished just two games back of the Dodgers.

The National League's Most Valuable Player Award was given to Willie in 1965. It was a so-so year for the "Say Hey" kid—52 home runs, 112 RBIs, and a .317 batting average.

That's what made the first coast-to-coast World Series, the Giants against their old neighbors, the Yankees, such a historic one. The Yanks, as always, were loaded. They had Mickey Mantle and Roger Maris in the lineup, and Whitey Ford and Ralph Terry, who'd led the league with 23 wins, on the mound. It promised to be a classic fall classic and it certainly was. The Giants lost game one at Candlestick, 6-2, but, to the delight of a howling home-town crowd at its first World Series, they took game two, 2-0, on a McCovey home run. Back in New York, the Yanks won game three, 3-2, with Bill Stafford tossing a four-hitter and Maris driving in two runs. Game four was tied going into the seventh when Hiller hit a grand slam, the first ever by a National Leaguer in World Series competition, and gave the Giants a 7-3 win. But—a dark omen—Marichal completed only four innings when his finger was smashed on an attempted bunt, and he was lost for the Series. New York won game five, 5-3, on a three-run homer by rookie Tom Tresh. Then, back at Candlestick, where game six was delayed for three days by rain, the Giants rallied and won, 5-2, as Cepeda nailed three hits.

Game seven was one of the best ever. The Yanks' Ralph Terry was in top form on the mound, pitching a two-hitter into the ninth to keep his team out front, 1-0. "You must remember that I was the goat of the last game of the Sixty series, giving up that home run to Mazeroski," pointed out Terry. "So in the last game of '62, I had a lot of atoning to do. I was never more pumped up in my whole life."

But the Giants had one final surge left from that fabulous 1962 season. In the bottom of the last inning, with the Giants down, 1-0, Matty Alou beat out a bunt and Mays hit a double. McCovey came up with two out and two on. Forty thousand people were on their feet. A mere single would give the Giants their first world championship in San Francisco.

The tall, muscular McCovey swung and hit a ripping line drive toward the right side of the infield. Fans started to yell. Mays and Alou began to run. The Giants players began to ascend the steps of their dugout . . .

. . . and second baseman Bobby Richardson caught the ball.

Despite the incredible disappointment of the Series loss, the strong Giants team pulled itself back together and started out the 1963 season with a lot of wins. Cepeda, now recognized as a superstar, hit .316 with 34 home runs. Mays had another great year with 38 home runs and a .314 average. And this was the year that McCovey, along with Milwaukee's Hank Aaron, led the league with 44 home runs.

But the Giants' story that year was not at the plate—it was on the mound. Juan Marichal, who had won 18 games in 1962, dominated the National League with his 25-8 record. The pitcher had been extraordinary from the moment he took the mound in 1960 and threw a one-hit

Pitcher Mike McCormick reminded the collector who obtained this shirt that he won the Cy Young Award in 1967, the year he posted a 22-10 record.

Below, a yearbook from 1966, when the team finished just a game and a half behind the Dodgers.

Below right, Willie's contract for the 1967 season, during which the Giants paid him $125,000.

shutout. He averaged 20 wins a year from 1962 to 1971, won 26 in 1968, pitched in eight All-Star Games, threw a no-hitter in 1963, and pitched 16 innings in one game the same year. His career record was 243-142, all but five wins for the Giants. Despite an ugly fight with the Dodgers' Johnny Roseboro in 1965—in an ongoing feud, Marichal hit the catcher over the head with a bat, setting off one of the major leagues' most violent brawls—he remained a popular player in San Francisco and was elected to the Hall of Fame in 1983.

But even Marichal's heroics couldn't keep the Giants on track in 1963, and they finished the season third to one of the strongest Dodgers teams ever. In 1964, the Giants, aided by Mays's 47 home runs, won 90 games—only to take fourth place to St. Louis in that year's talent-loaded National League. In 1965, they won 95 games, including 22 of the last 30. That was the year Mays ended up homering 52 times to lead the majors, placing eleventh on the all-time single-season list. McCovey hit 39 homers himself, but the

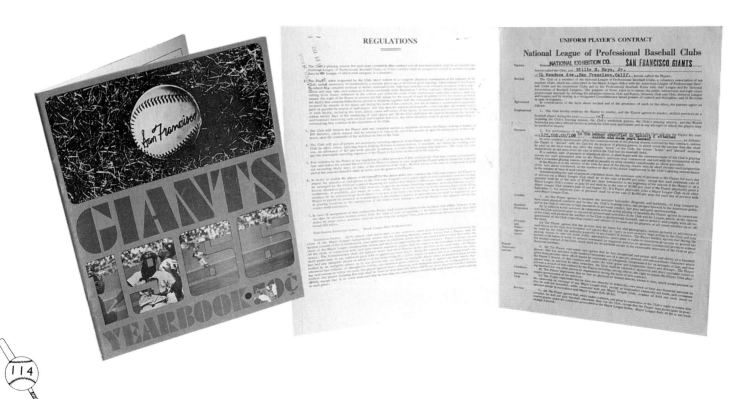

Pitching ace Juan Marichal, who won his very first game on a one-hitter and from 1962 to 1970 averaged 20 wins a year.

bats were not enough. The Dodgers managed to take 97 games—Koufax and Drysdale between them brought in 49—and went on to meet Minnesota in the World Series.

Things continued in the same vein in 1966. The Giants won 93 games and still finished second, again to the Dodgers. In 1967 they posted 91 wins and *still* came in second, 10½ back of the amazing St.

115

Before the second Giants game I ever went to, I marched down to the fence where I saw Orlando Cepeda, Felipe Alou, and Ramon Monzant playing pepper. I think I was 11. I was scared to death and I knew they wouldn't sign my program. Well, they not only signed, but they actually talked to me. I was thrilled. I've been a die-hard Giants fan ever since.

—DUANE GARRETT, 44, of Sausalito

Louis Cardinals. In 1968 it was the same old story—88 wins, helped along by McCovey's league-leading 36 homers and 105 RBIs, and another second-place finish, St. Louis once more out in front.

In 1969, with both leagues newly expanded and split into Eastern and Western divisions, the Giants again won 90 games and finished second in their division, this time to Atlanta, who was helped along by another 44-homer year from Hank Aaron. In 1970, the Giants won 86 games and came in third to the Cincinnati Reds.

Finally, after averaging 90 wins a year for ten years and hanging only one pennant on the wall to show for it, the Giants finished first in the division in 1971. Under their new manager, Charlie Fox, they won

Three-hundred-game winner Gaylord Perry in his Giants years.

90 games and beat out the Dodgers by a single match. The team had faltered in September, though, losing 19 of 26 games, and was still weak when the divisional play-off against Pittsburgh began. The Pirates won the pennant.

Perhaps no team in baseball history has played as well as the 1960s Giants. They won 909 games from 1961 through 1970. Their roster was studded with future Hall of Famers—Cepeda, Marichal, Mays, McCovey. Other great All-Stars included Golden Glove third baseman Jim Davenport; 30-30 club specialist Bobby Bonds, the only player in modern baseball history to hit a grand slam in his first at-bat in the majors (and against the Dodgers, no less); Gaylord Perry, who pitched 134 winning games for the Giants and went on to become the only pitcher to win Cy Young Awards in both leagues; Mike McCormick, who in 1967 led the league in wins and picked up the Comeback Player of the Year award along with his Cy Young; the feisty Alou brothers, Felipe and Matty; and Jim Ray Hart, who during a late-season game in 1970 hit for the cycle and drove in six RBIs in one inning to tie the major league record. It may be that no team has ever had so much talent and worked so hard and come away with so little to show for it.

CHAPTER FIVE

THE LURIE ERA
The Seventies and Eighties

After the 1971 divisional championship, the Giants fell apart. The team plunged to fifth, a rousing 26½ games out, in 1972. They made a mild recovery in 1973—11 games out, third place—then crashed into a horrendous slump that saw them finish 30 games out in 1974 and 27½ out in 1975. Fans had flocked to Candlestick Park in its first seven years, an average of 1.5 million each season, but now they abandoned the team. Attendance in 1974 and 1975 averaged a pathetic 7,000 per game—exactly half the numbers that had attended during the championship season of 1971. The mighty Giants, pillars of the National League since the 1880s, had reached their lowest moment. The Stonehams, fed up, announced that they'd begun talks to move the team out of San Francisco to Minnesota.

In stepped a fan, businessman Bob Lurie, who had started going to Giants games the first week the team arrived at Seals Stadium. Unable to influence city officials or other businessmen to help keep the club in town, he decided to buy it.

"It was the craziest deal of all time," the well-tanned Lurie said, smiling easily and remembering that hectic period as he relaxed in his office. "I was partners with [Bob] Short [a Washington, D.C., businessman], and we were going to buy the team for $8 million

Opposite, the Giants celebrate their 1989 pennant, the first in 17 years. Pitcher Dave Drevecky *(second from left)* refractured his left arm in the hubbub.

119

In 1971 the Giants
finished a lowly
seventh.

Mays wore these
spikes in the 1971
season.

and everything was set. Then I suddenly lost Bob as a partner. I didn't even have the whole $8 million and the whole deal was going to fall through. The major league owners, when they heard of my problem, said 'OK, you have five hours to raise the money.' Is that nuts or what?"

Lurie leaned forward on his large desk, still marveling at the course of events over twenty years later. "I called every politician and businessman in San Francisco and nobody would help me. Then, about a half hour before the deadline, when it looked hopeless, a guy from Arizona calls. He told my secretary he had the money and wanted to be of help. I never met this guy in my life. I talked to him, called his bank, where people assured me he was recklessly rich, and called back the Stonehams. That afternoon we bought the San Francisco Giants."

Two years later, in 1978, Lurie bought out the Arizonan, Bud Herseth, and became sole owner. Meanwhile he'd begun the process of rebuilding the team and its attendance. Using sophisticated marketing methods and heavy promotion throughout the San Francisco area, he sold an average of 1.1 million tickets each year from 1977 to 1985. The team became financially stable.

On the field, however, the Giants continued to disappoint. Lurie hired and

Die-hard fan Bob Lurie, convinced the Giants would flee the Bay Area for Minnesota, bought the team in 1976.

fired five managers in his first ten years in the front office, always seeking a winning combination and rarely getting it. Despite the best efforts of managers Bill Rigney, who was brought back for the 1976 season, Joe Altobelli, Dave Bristol, Frank Robinson, and Danny Ozark, the team had only three winning seasons in the first nine years of Lurie's reign and never finished better than third in their division.

The Giants hit rock bottom in 1984 when the team lost an incredible 96 games. Fans said the Giants couldn't get worse, but they did, and quickly. Off to a flying start in April 1985, they proceeded to lose 100 games for the season, the only time any Giants team, even in the good old days of Buck Ewing & Company, lost a century of games. Things were so bad that during the hundredth loss the fans at the Stick were cheering for the Braves to win it, thereby insuring the Giants' immortality.

Incapable of finding the solution to his woes, Lurie turned to old friend Al Rosen, who was very happy being general manager of the Houston Astros at the time. The two met that summer. They met again in the fall. They met again and again and again. They talked of winning and losing, managers and coaches, fans and supporters.

"I knew that the only way out of our situation was to go with baseball men—men who knew the game and knew the players. Rosen was the right man for the chief executive slot, no doubt about it. There's no finer baseball executive in America," recalled Lurie. "But what we

Bobby Bonds hit a grand slam home run in his very first at bat for the Giants in 1968. In his seven seasons there he went on to become **one of the Giants' premier sluggers, hitting 32 homers in 1969 and 39 in 1973.** **This signed jersey was worn by the popular Bobby Bonds, who hit 332 home runs in his long career with the Giants, which lasted from 1968 to 1974.**

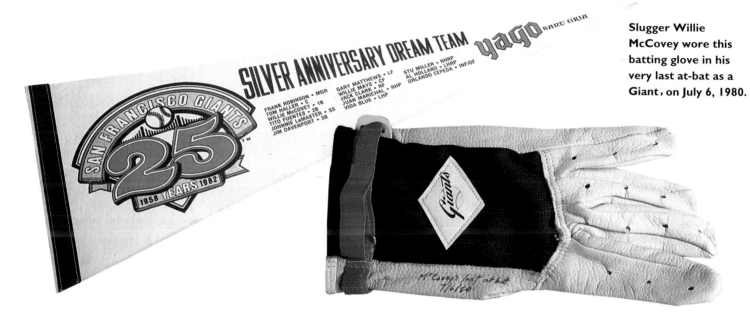

SILVER ANNIVERSARY DREAM TEAM

SAN FRANCISCO GIANTS
25 YEARS 1958 1982

FRANK ROBINSON • MGR
TOM HALLER • C
WILLIE McCOVEY • 1B
TITO FUENTES • 2B
JOHNNIE LAMASTER • 3B
JIM DAVENPORT • 3B

GARY MATTHEWS • LF
WILLIE MAYS • CF
JACK CLARK • RF
JUAN MARICHAL • RHP
VIDA BLUE • LHP

STU MILLER • RHRP
AL HOLLAND • LHRP
ORLANDO CEPEDA • INF/OF

yago SANT GRUA

Slugger Willie
McCovey wore this
batting glove in his
very last at-bat as a
Giant, on July 6, 1980.

The twenty-fifth-anniversary dream team included McCovey, Mays, Cepeda, and Marichal.

really needed was a top manager, a manager who could whip players into a fighting team. I just didn't know what to do. We had some capable guys, people like Bill Rigney and Frank Robinson, but nothing worked."

The man Rosen and Lurie turned to was journeyman coach and manager Roger Craig, a hot and cold ex-pitcher who clinched a World Series one year with the Dodgers and lost 46 games in two years with the Mets. Craig had bounced around baseball since his retiring as a player, serving as pitching coach for the Detroit Tigers and San Diego Padres and, for two years, as Padres manager.

A glove McCovey used in the 1970s.

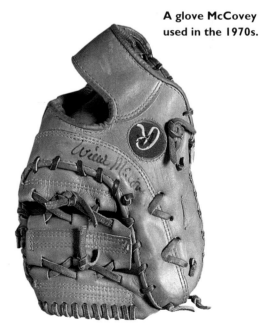

Above, manager Roger Craig's jersey. Few remember that the successful skipper posted one of the worst pitching records in baseball in 1962, when he went 10-24 for the hapless Mets.

Above right, Craig himself, whose tenure lasted from 1986 to 1992.

"After I met him a few times I knew he was the guy," declared Lurie. "He was a baseball man. Here's a guy who played in the big leagues for 13 years, coached pitchers for a decade, managed different minor league teams, and had two decent years with the Padres as manager. The most important thing, though, is that the players Al [Rosen] talked to all said Craig was a guy ballplayers respected. We needed that."

Craig proved everybody right. In 1986, his first full season as skipper of the Giants, the team won 83 games, up from 62 the year before, and finished third. Among Craig's achievements that year was the development of pitcher Mike Krukow, who'd always had trouble completing games. Krukow's 20-win season was the first for the Giants since 1973, when Ron Bryant had posted 24. In 1987, to the astonishment of San Franciscans from Sausalito to Carmel, the Giants won 90 games and took the divisional title. Much of their success was due to Craig's no-nonsense approach, the respect of his players, and Rosen's off-season trades.

Eager to get rid of deadwood, Rosen had traded away nearly a dozen Giants he was not happy with, making room for new acquisitions, and, more importantly, young players he and Craig were determined to bring up from the minors. Two superstars, Will Clark and Robby Thompson, were moved up fast and appeared on the opening-day roster in 1986. The next year, Rosen, the consummate swapper, made a sensational red, white, and blue trade on the Fourth of July, acquiring Kevin Mitchell, Dave Dravecky, and Craig Lefferts.

The 1987 team, one of the strongest the Giants had fielded since the 1954 world champs, won their division by a healthy six games. It was a team of powerhouse bats that more than made up for an erratic pitching staff, whose leader Mike LaCoss picked up just 13 wins. First baseman Will Clark, who had established himself as a star in 1986 with a .287 average and 11 home runs, was now weighing in as one of baseball's premier sluggers with a .308 average and 35 home runs. Jose Uribe hit .291. Candy Maldonado hit .292 with 20 home runs. Jeffrey Leonard clouted 19 home runs and Chili Davis 24. Kevin Mitchell, getting warmed up for bigger things, hit 15 homers with a .306 average, and Mike Aldrete batted .325. Meanwhile, 21-year-old rookie Matt Williams was learning the ropes, gearing up for back-to-back 30-plus homer seasons in 1990 and 1991.

The fans at Candlestick were hoping for a World Series that year, but the rugged St. Louis Cardinals would not fold under the Giants' relentless attack. The League Championship Series went the full seven games, with three of the Cardinals' four wins coming by a margin of two runs or less.

The Giants, never able to savor success, promptly busted in 1988, tumbling all the way to fourth in the division, 11½ games behind the red-hot Dodgers, who

A Seventies pennant.

Below, superstar Joe Morgan played for the Giants for two seasons and wore these cleats in his last game for San Francisco.

Above, this jersey was worn by second baseman Tito Fuentes in 1977. Although he was a fine player, he appears in the record books as the only man hit by a pitch three times in one game.

A beribboned button from the Seventies.

went on to win a dramatic World Series over the Oakland A's. Meanwhile, Rosen had been hard at work, acquiring Brett Butler to play center field. The steady, solid-hitting Butler was a real asset in the 1989 pennant drive spearheaded by Kevin Mitchell and Will Clark, who both had monster seasons.

Mitchell's sensational year has been compared to the great seasons of Mays, McCovey, Cepeda, Ott, and Terry. Batting .291, he hit 47 homers and knocked in

Jack Clark slides home in a 1979 game.

125 RBIs to lead the majors in both stats. "He was big, strong, and powerful," explained Mitchell's batting coach, former All-Star Dusty Baker. "Until '89 he had not realized his potential. That season he did. He realized, mentally, that his physical capabilities were enormous. He's the one Giant, I think, who has the true potential to have career numbers like McCovey and Cepeda."

Clark's bat was almost as hot that season—he had 23 homers, 111 RBIs, averaged .333, and led the league with his

Catcher Bob Brenly's equipment from the 1985 season.

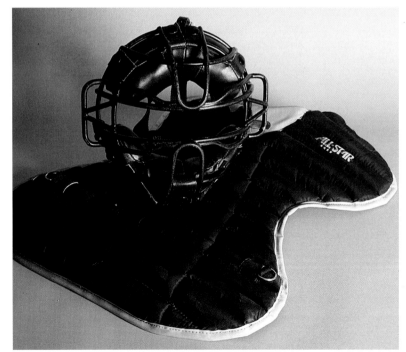

104 runs—and so was his glove, with 1,445 putouts. The first baseman was establishing himself as a solid, consistent hitter who could hit for power and average and who could be depended on in the toughest situations in a game.

Clark, Mitchell, and Butler were not the only players who excelled in 1988 and 1989. In both years three Giants were selected for the All-Star team. Pitcher Rick Reuschel, in the middle of a 19-win season, and second baseman Robby Thompson joined Clark in 1988, and Reuschel returned with Clark and Mitchell in 1989.

Determined to make it to the 1989 World Series, the Giants outpaced the Padres by three games to get to the league playoffs against Chicago, then beat up on the Cubs four games to one. Will the Thrill Clark, who averaged .650 with 13 hits in the Series, generated thunder in game one when he went four for four, homered twice, and drove in six runs to set a new playoff record. That series more than anything else established Clark as one of the great players of the Giants' modern era.

With the pennant safely in hand, the Giants prepared to go up against the Oakland A's from across the bay for the world championship. Little did they, or the muscular Athletics, imagine that the Series would turn out to be one of the strangest ever held.

Below, Robby Thompson's jersey. The second baseman was runnerup to Todd Worrell for 1986 Rookie-of-the-Year honors.

The 1989 Series was a bonanza for baseball, even though it featured two teams in adjacent towns. Television networks normally hate too much proximity because it limits viewership to one area instead of spreading it across the country. TV especially likes anything-East-Coast versus anything-West-Coast. But in the Giants and the Athletics, baseball had a super Series. The Giants, strong since

1987, had been knocking on the world championship door and seemed poised to push it in. The Athletics were *the* glamour team in baseball with the home run twins, Jose Canseco and Mark McGwire, pitching sensation Dave Stewart, and likable Tony La Russa, the manager who was also a lawyer. Television also got sensational pictures of the legendary San Francisco streets for its viewers.

This flag celebrated the 1987 divisional championship, which came just two years after the team had finished in last place. The loss of the pennant to the Cards crushed fans.

The bottom flag was manufactured by a local optimist just before the Giants lost the pennant in 1987.

I have always loved baseball. I moved here 16 years ago and naturally started coming to games. I think the Giants are a good team because they just don't give up. There won't be a generational bridge, though. My kids are hopeless A's fans.

—KARA FLETCHER, of Upper Portola Valley

I like the Giants because they are always in it, win or lose. They're up, they're down, but they're always playing hard. That's all any fan wants, that his guys try.
—WILLIAM QUITALIG, 27, of Milpitas

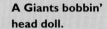
A Giants bobbin' head doll.

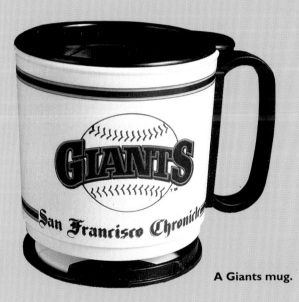
A Giants mug.

People *never* thought the Giants would actually leave. When we came within an inch of losing them to Florida, I think people finally woke up. Now, the Giants will get the new stadium they need and I think a new stadium will kick off a whole new era for the Giants here. It's like romance. You don't realize how much you love someone until you almost lose them.
—JEAN CHAGNIOT, 34, of San Francisco

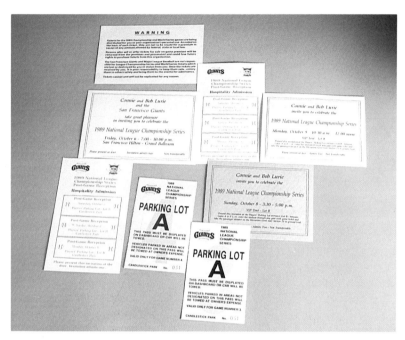

Invitations and passes to the preplayoff parties in 1989.

Everyone looked forward to a wonderful Series—lots of home runs, lots of strikeouts, lots of between-innings pictures of seals at Golden Gate Park and cable cars. What they got was something else.

Baseball games have been rained out. They have been canceled or postponed because of snowstorms, hurricanes, fog, and even bugs. But never an earthquake. Not an earthquake. Yet that's just what happened to the 1989 Bay Area World Series. What transpired on the field made it a nightmare for the Giants, and what happened off the field, or rather under the field, made it a nightmare for everybody else.

No one on the Giants thought earthquake when the Series started in Oakland against the powerful A's. The ground was rumbling, but only because the A's kept running over it, mainly the home plate part of it. The Oakland bashers, led by Jose Canseco, swamped the Giants in game one, 5-0, and pounded them again in game two, 5-1. The San Franciscans were hoping that their return to wind-buffeted Candlestick might turn their luck around.

That third game, on October 17, was scheduled for a warm and pleasant night. Shortly after 5:00 P.M. thousands of fans were in their seats and players were warming up on the field. Then it hit.

At 5:04 the earthquake, whose epicenter was 50 miles south of San Francisco, rumbled through the Bay Area. It knocked down the Oakland Bay Bridge, destroyed hundreds of homes, completely collapsed a highway, killed 59 people, started roaring fires that destroyed millions of dollars worth of property, and knocked out power for hours throughout northern sections of California.

Up in the private booths, few realized it hit.

"I was writing a letter to a friend and I felt the table move a little, but not much. I kept writing. All of a sudden all of the power went and I thought . . . uh, oh. . . ." said fan Duane Garret.

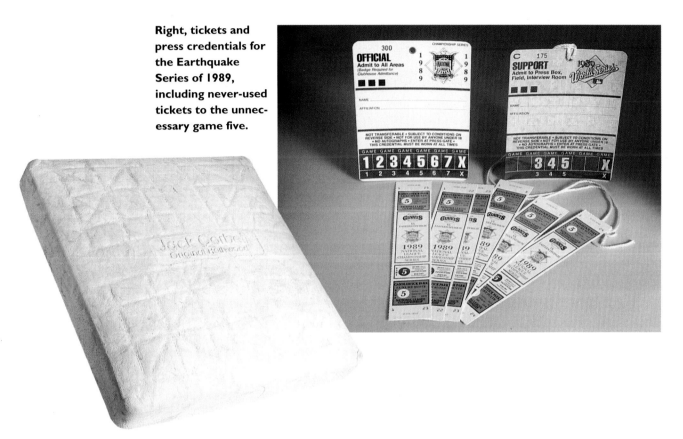

Right, tickets and press credentials for the Earthquake Series of 1989, including never-used tickets to the unnecessary game five.

A collector wound up with this second base from one of the 1989 World Series games at Candlestick.

Kathryn Gordon, a college student, was taken to the game by her family as a birthday present. Standing outside the park recently, in her white, orange, and black Giants tee shirt and Giants hat, her long sandy hair tumbling out of it, she remembered the night vividly.

"We had seats in the extra seat pavilion that they pull down and out for sellouts in centerfield. It's one of those metal bottom sections and when someone just walks down the aisle the whole place rumbles a bit. So I'm sitting there and suddenly there's this terrific rumbling noise and the whole section shakes and I'm thinking this is a group of six guys running down the steps. I put it out of my mind. I was staring at the field. Suddenly, the whole field started to move up and down and my soda and program and everything I had went flying," she said.

Players yelled for their wives to come down to the field to avoid the danger of falling objects. Fans scrambled to get out.

133

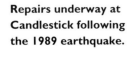

Repairs underway at Candlestick following the 1989 earthquake.

134

The Giants, quickly using auxiliary generators, restored much of the light knocked out by the quake. Announcers quickly restored order.

"There was no panic. No stampeding, nothing you might expect," said restaurant owner Joe Alioto, who was at the game. "The fans were great. We were all concerned and worried, particularly if you had family in town because you didn't know what happened to the town then. But the fans were terrific. A lot of injuries didn't happen because the fans were so good."

Miraculously, little damage was suffered at Candlestick. Longtime critics of the park probably expected it to simply fall

down. If it couldn't take wind, how could it take an earthquake? But except for a few chunks of concrete that fell, it held up well, a tribute to its architects, who explained later that they had designed it with a little flex and leeway because it was in earthquake country. To be on the safe side, Commissioner Fay Vincent decided the third game of the Series would not be played until numerous inspections showed Candlestick absolutely safe. That took ten days.

The delay did not help the Giants. They immediately dropped game three by a 13 to 7 margin and then lost the fourth and final game of the sweep, 9-6

"I had nothing but bad feelings about that Series," said owner Bob Lurie. "I felt terrible about the earthquake and the people killed and injured and all the damage it caused, of course, and I felt awful that we had a very good team which had a very good year and got swept in the Series. Not a good October, not at all," he said.

The Giants had climbed to within sight of the peak of the world championship mountain, but they didn't make it all the way. The following year they slipped to third, six games out, and fell to fourth the next year. Kevin Mitchell was traded. Dave Dravecky lost his arm. The owners vowed to leave Candlestick. The Nineties would be a different era.

The batting helmet of Will Clark, one of the most consistent superstars in the game.

135

TODAY'S GIANTS

The contemporary Giants, the Giants of principal owner Peter Magowan and general manager Bob Quinn, are a team with talent, power, and drive, with strong hitters, good fielders, and pitchers who are sometimes wonderful and sometimes shaky. They are, in many ways, a manager's dream. John McGraw would have loved their talent. Bill Terry would have loved their precision and work ethic. And Leo Durocher would have loved their team spirit.

The Giants have earned the respect of everyone. "They are, year in and year out, one of the two or three toughest teams in their division," said Frank Viola, the Red Sox pitcher who has faced them over and over. "Clark and Williams are two of the most dangerous hitters in all of baseball. They hit for both average and power and they are clutch hitters. The overall team is good, but those guys are lethal. I had to work very hard to keep ahead on the count with them. You can't be 3-0, 3-1 on those guys. If you take it easy, they'll get you."

Dodgers skipper Tommy Lasorda is always wary when he sees the Giants' colors. "If I see black and orange signs in a restaurant, I get nervous," he admitted. "That team is good, every year. They always have good hitting, always have good pitching, and they never let up. Never. Someone will say, 'Oh, look, the Giants are ten behind.' I tell them wait

Will Clark steps into the batter's box. When he's finished, Clark may well be in the Hall of Fame.

The glove of Kevin Mitchell.

Below, a 1990 team ball featuring the beloved Dave Dravecky's sig at the top along with Kevin Mitchell's and Will Clark's at the bottom.

Powerhouse Matt Williams.

I never patterned my swing after anybody else. People kept telling me I should, but I never did. Who am I going to copy, Willie Mays? Nobody can hit like Willie Mays.

—MATT WILLIAMS, Giants

138

Slugger Kevin Mitchell hit 47 home runs in 1989 and 35 in 1990, but was sent to Seattle in a trade that stunned fans.

two weeks and they'll be three or four behind. Wait two months and people will be behind them. They're a great ball club."

The players themselves are a confident group, but a group that realizes that teams win games, not players. When each of them talks about the Giants, it's always about the team, not about themselves. And there are no apologists in the clubhouse. If the hitters or the pitchers aren't pulling their weight, they're the first to admit it.

"The press and the fans keep saying we haven't had good pitching over the last few years. That's simply not true," said Matt Williams, his massive shoulders stretching against his jersey as he practiced his swing. "You look at our schedule and you'll see lots of 1-0, 3-2 games. Our pitchers often do the job but the hitters don't come through. The hitters have to produce for their pitchers."

Williams, who can hit for the average and hit in the clutch, has become one of the team's best home run producers. "I think he's one of the best power hitters in baseball," declared Montreal's veteran catcher Gary Carter, who played with Williams one season. "I think he's going to have even better years in the future."

Kevin Mitchell was the workhorse on the Eighties team. He was a huge, bulky man whose oddly shaped body carries so much poundage around the hips you'd

139

Souvenir watch from
Candlestick.

Pitcher Dave Dravecky wore this jersey the year before he lost his arm to cancer.

Kevin Mitchell's hat.

never take him for an all-around player. But he was. When Mitchell arrived from the Mets he was basically a singles hitter, but maturity, and help from Willie Mays, turned him into a slugger. His trade to Seattle stunned fans.

And then, of course, there's "the Natural," "the Thrill"—first baseman Will Clark, who was a national sensation before he even finished high school. A college All-American three years in a row, a star for the 1984 Olympic team, and the number two draft pick in 1985, Clark was impressive as a rookie, and has remained Mr. Consistency for the Giants.

"Really?" asked Clark, bootblack smeared under his eyes as he sat in a hot dugout waiting his turn in the batting cage. "I don't listen to any of that stuff. My job is to come to the ballpark and hit. I have to get on base or knock in somebody who's already on base. It's all that simple."

The Giants are a team of great heart with fans who who have great hearts. There was no better example of this than the heroic tale of Dave Dravecky. In 1988 the good-looking star pitcher developed cancer in his pitching arm. The arm broke and he should never have pitched again. Undaunted, Dravecky worked hard to

140

The sad end of pitcher Dave Dravecky's career. The gutsy hurler thought he had recovered from cancer and returned to pitching, but in his second start in 1989 his arm snapped; he later lost it.

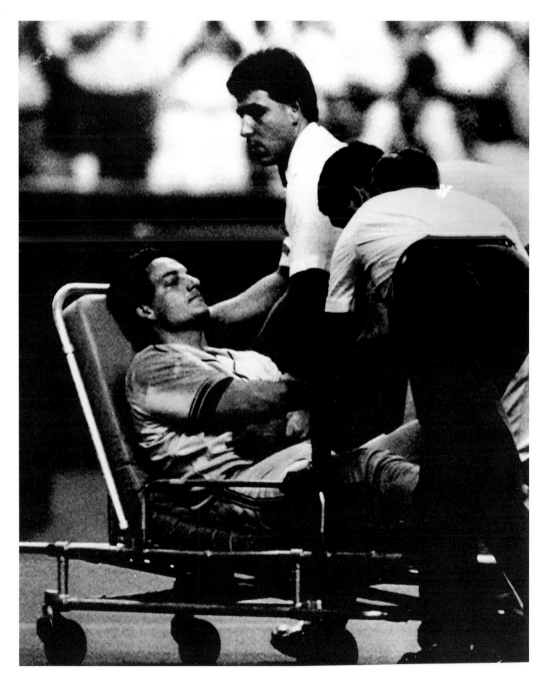

Will Clark is the best first baseman in baseball. He loves to play and it really shows. I like his style. He's always playing his heart out. He shouldn't strike out so much, though. He'd be a lot better off getting doubles than striking out.

—JAMON ACKER, 11, of Fresno

A Will Clark Candlestick giveaway wristband.

rehabilitate his cancerous arm and, against all odds, returned to pitch at Candlestick midway through the 1989 season. Just for taking the mound he was greeted with a rousing, standing ovation equal to that at any World Series. Amazingly, he won the game and was treated to another round of cheers when he left the field. He went on to post a second win and then, under the stress of repeated hurling, the bone suddenly snapped in the midst of a throw; eventually he lost the arm.

With that kind of spirit behind them, the Giants' future looks bright, but winning pennants in the major leagues is not easy. "One factor people don't take into consideration, and I'm not using this as a crutch, is that we play in the toughest, most talented division in all of baseball," said catcher Terry Kennedy, his bat leaning against his knee. "Look, for us to win a divisional title we've got to get by the Dodgers. That's a major job right there.

The Dodgers are always good. And then there's Cincinnati, always tough, and San Diego. And in '91 Atlanta jumped right out of the pack at everybody."

Despite the 35 long years since the team moved West, the Giants still maintain a strong historical tradition going back to their New York days. Most of the retired names painted on the outfield walls—Mathewson (*), McGraw (*), Terry (3), Ott (4), Hubbell (11), Mays (24), Marichal (27), McCovey (44)—belong to New York players. On the walls of the executive offices are handsomely carved busts of Buck Ewing, Iron Man Joe McGinnity, John McGraw, Bill Terry, and Roger Bresnahan. An enormous black-and-white picture of Christy Mathewson, the largest in the office, graces another wall. The players, too, more than most, are aware of the tradition.

"I grew up in Mel Ott's hometown and all I ever heard people talk about were the Giants. My whole childhood: the Giants, the Giants, the Giants," explained Will Clark. "Here at Candlestick you can't avoid that tradition. You run into the outfield and you see all the retired numbers on the wall. You go to spring training and Willie Mays is there to help you. The clubhouse is full of pictures of the Giants of days gone by. This is a traditional club and

*Numbers were not used until 1929.

A twilight view of the ballpark from the other side of San Francisco Bay.

I'm glad it is. There's something more to baseball, really, than just playing tonight's game. You look at those numbers on the fence when you trot out there to play and all that history comes at you."

The Giants of the Nineties remain a team full of questions. Can deeper pitching be found? Can Williams continue to hit the National League pitchers as hard as he has in the last few years? Can Clark become one of the great first basemen of all time?

Can the National League West possibly get any tougher?

And, most important of all, what will the new owners be like and will they be able to get a new ballpark built? Fans and players have always complained that Candlestick Park was inadequate and for years previous owner Bob Lurie unsuccessfully tried to get support for a new stadium. Frustrated, he then contracted to sell his team to a group from Saint

143

I grew up in Mel Ott's home town, so ever since I was a kid I knew all about the Giants. When you get here you hear all the stories, and not just about Juan and Willie and Cepeda and McCovey. You hear all about Christy Mathewson and John McGraw, too. You walk on the field and there are those retired number insignias staring at you on the outfield wall. You can't escape the great tradition of this team. This team has played over 100 years of baseball. That's just amazing.

—WILL CLARK, Giants

The Thrill's jersey.

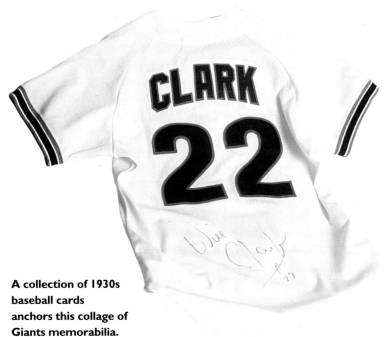

A collection of 1930s baseball cards anchors this collage of Giants memorabilia.

Petersburg, Florida. Suddenly aware that they might lose the team, area fans rallied to support the ball club. The league, too, wanted the Giants in San Francisco and eventually forced Lurie to sell locally for $100 million ($92 million more than he paid). Led by Peter Magowan, chairman of Safeway, a local group has now brought in a whole new management team. Will Magowan have more luck in getting a new park? Will MVP-winner Barry Bonds produce? Will general manager Bob Quinn have more success than Al Rosen in rebuilding the team? Will the new manager be able to bring a World Series flag to San Francisco, something Roger Craig could never do?

Fans are hoping that the new owners will get a new stadium built, but no matter where around the Bay they play, the Giants will always be the Giants. Their history and tradition will go with them, whether it's to downtown San Francisco or to a nearby suburb. Old Smiling Mickey Welch wouldn't care where the team takes the field when the last notes of the national anthem fade into the night. Neither would Highpockets Kelly, or Muggsy McGraw, or Carl Hubbell, or Bobby Thomson, or the Willies, or Juan, or the Baby Bull—just as long as there's a nice green field, excited kids leaning over the rail for autographs, the smell of peanuts, and lots of fans on a warm summer night.

GIANT GREATS

ORLANDO CEPEDA

The "Baby Bull" was one of the strongest hitters in National League history, a reputation he established in his very first game in 1958 when he crushed a home run off Don Drysdale. That year he went on to win Rookie of the Year honors with 25 homers and a .312 average. Nine times he hit .300 and eight times he crashed 25 homers or more. He was injured in 1965 and traded.

Cepeda was vitally important to the Giants because he joined the team during their very first season in San Francisco. During his first few years the home-grown California star helped break the old ties with New York and established the franchise on the West Coast. Many believe a jail term for marijuana smuggling has kept Cepeda out of the Hall of Fame.

WILL CLARK

They call him "the Thrill" and "the Natural." Sportswriters have said he was the greatest college player of all time, and tee shirts with his portrait have sold better than those of any other Giant in history. With his erect stance, Clark has a natural feel for the pitch and always seems to make contact.

Clark, the number two pick in the 1985 draft, homered in his first at-bat in the minors and his first in the majors—and off Nolan Ryan, no less. After an impressive rookie year, he averaged .308 with 35 homers in 1987 to lead San Francisco to a division title. Clark has been a consistent All-Star and has established himself as a regular .300 hitter. He hit a smoking .650 in the 1989 League Championship Series.

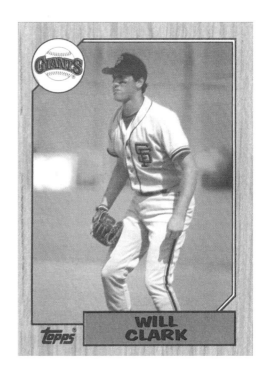

WILL CLARK

Monte Irvin

It is heartbreaking to think what Monte Irvin, one of the greatest athletes this country has produced, would have done in the majors if there had been no color line. A four-sport star in high school, he played for the Negro Leagues' Newark Eagles for eight years before the Giants signed him in 1949. He hit .422 in 1940 and .396 in 1941. After serving in the army during the war, he played himself back into shape in the Puerto Rican Winter League, earning MVP honors there, then came back to Newark and helped the team win the Colored World Series in 1946. When he signed with the Giants they put him in Triple A, but in 1950, after hitting .510 with ten home runs in 18 games, he was called up permanently. He hit .299 in New York, then went on a tear in 1951, hitting .312 with 24 home runs during the regular season and .458 in the World Series. Injured in 1952, he never regained his form. He was elected to the Hall of Fame in 1973.

MONTE IRVIN
OUTFIELDER

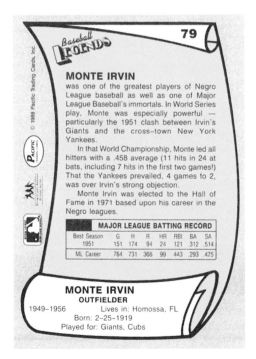

79

MONTE IRVIN
was one of the greatest players of Negro League baseball as well as one of Major League Baseball's immortals. In World Series play, Monte was especially powerful — particularly the 1951 clash between Irvin's Giants and the cross-town New York Yankees.

In that World Championship, Monte led all hitters with a .458 average (11 hits in 24 at bats, including 7 hits in the first two games!) That the Yankees prevailed, 4 games to 2, was over Irvin's strong objection.

Monte Irvin was elected to the Hall of Fame in 1971 based upon his career in the Negro leagues.

MAJOR LEAGUE BATTING RECORD							
Best Season	G	H	R	HR	RBI	BA	SA
1951	151	174	94	24	121	.312	.514
ML Career	764	731	366	99	443	.293	.475

MONTE IRVIN
OUTFIELDER
1949–1956   Lives in: Homossa, FL
Born: 2-25-1919
Played for: Giants, Cubs

Iron Man McGinnity

Iron Man Joe McGinnity (he was an iron worker in the off-season) was one of the most durable pitchers in history. The turn-of-the-century hurler didn't get to the majors until he was 28, then played just ten seasons, but he was impressive. After playing for Brooklyn and Baltimore, McGinnity moved to the Giants in 1902, and there he and Christy Mathewson formed a one-two punch unmatched in baseball history. One or the other of them led the league in wins from 1903 to 1908. Iron Man won 31 games in 1903, 35 in 1904, and 27 in 1906. A glutton for the ball, he often pitched both ends of doubleheaders, once racking up five wins in six days. He often served as a reliever, too, and for seven straight years played in more games than any other pitcher. McGinnity was elected to the Hall of Fame in 1946.

147

JUAN MARICHAL

The high-kicking hurler from the Dominican Republic was good even from the start—so good that he won his first Giants game on a one-hit shutout and in his next delivered a four-hitter to the world champion Pittsburgh Pirates. Juan averaged 22 wins a year over a seven-year stretch and wound up with a 243-142 record.

Marichal was a crowd favorite. He won with hits and he won without them, posting many 1-0 and 2-0 decisions. The aftermath of a severe penicillin reaction in 1970—chronic arthritis and back pain, which would have ruined most men—led him to retool his repertoire and eliminate his fastball. He came back to win 18 in 1971. One of the top prospects ever to come out of the Caribbean, Marichal helped open the door for other Latin American players. He was elected to the Hall of Fame in 1983.

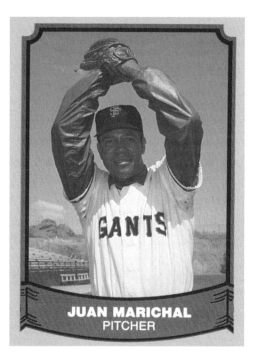

JUAN MARICHAL
PITCHER

MATHEWSON, NEW YORK - NATIONALS

CHRISTY MATHEWSON

Perhaps the greatest pure pitcher in baseball history, Mathewson had an uncanny memory for batters' weaknesses and an unhittable screwball. But his lasting impact on the game had as much to do with his demeanor and background as with his extraordinary skills. College educated, a genuine sportsman, and a refined gentleman, Matty was the main reason thousands of women and children started attending games in the early 1900s.

Mathewson won a total of 373 games, 30 or more in three straight years, and never fewer than 22 from 1903 to 1914. His three shutouts in the 1905 World Series set a single-series record that's never been approached. He had remarkable control, even of his screwball, and was able to finish most games with fewer than 100 pitches and in under 90 minutes.

Joining the military during World War I, Mathewson was gassed in Europe and never fully recovered. At the age of 45, while listening to the World Series on the radio, he died of tuberculosis brought on by the gas. He was elected to the Hall of Fame in 1936.

WILLIE MAYS

Willie Mays was one of the greatest sluggers in baseball history with 660 homes runs, 1,903 RBIs, and a .302 lifetime major league average. As a fielder, he made the act of routinely catching a fly ball a three-act drama with his long runs, hat flying, and his wonderful basket catches.

Mays was a walking (or in his case always running) atlas of baseball. Many stars played for several teams and some for many teams, but Willie Mays thrilled people all over. As a 15 year old kid he came up as a star in the Negro Leagues (with the Birmingham Black Barons) and then played a month in Minneapolis, where he hit .477. He then moved to the Giants, playing with them in New York and in San Francisco. In addition, Mays played winter ball in Puerto Rico for a number of years. Finally he came back to New York to end his career with the Mets. No matter where people saw him play, though, they'll all remember him as the player who was forever young, as the "Say Hey" kid.

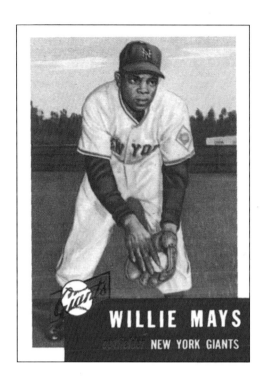

WILLIE MAYS
NEW YORK GIANTS

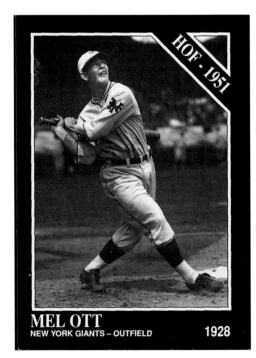

MEL OTT
NEW YORK GIANTS – OUTFIELD   1928

MEL OTT

Ott was a raw 17-year-old teenager when he was signed by the Giants. Unwilling to let minor league manager Casey Stengel tamper with him, McGraw had Ott sit next to him on the Giants bench for two years—just to look and listen. In 1928 he was put into the lineup for good at age 19.

Despite his odd foot-in-the-bucket swing, Ott went on to be one of the great hitters in major league history with 511 home runs, a .304 batting average, and 1,860 RBIs. In his time, he was as revered as Ruth. His home run production was so prodigious that it wasn't until two generations had passed, in 1967, that Willie Mays finally broke his National League 511 homer record. A favorite of fans and press, with his Southern charm and gracious manners, Ott was dubbed "Master Melvin" and "Mellifluous Melvin."

149

GIANT STATS

GIANTS ALL-TIME PITCHING LEADERS

WINS

Mathewson	372
Hubbell	253
Marichal	238
Fitzsimmons	170
Schumacher	158
McGinnity	151
Wiltse	136
Perry	134
Jansen	120
Tesreau	115

GAMES

Lavelle	647
Mathewson	634
Minton	552
Hubbell	535
Moffitt	459
Marichal	458
Fitzsimmons	403
Barr	394
Schumacher	391
Perry	367

SAVES

Lavelle	127
Minton	125
Moffitt	83
Linzy	77
Garrelts	48
Miller	46
McMahon	36
Lefferts	35
J. Johnson	29
Sosa	27

INNINGS

Mathewson	4772
Hubbell	3591
Marichal	3443
Fitzsimmons	2515
Schumacher	2483
Perry	2295
McGinnity	2151
Wiltse	2050
Ames	1944
Taylor	1853

STRIKEOUTS

Mathewson	2502
Marichal	2281
Hubbell	1677
Perry	1606
Ames	1118
McCormick	1030
Bolin	977
Wiltse	948
Antonelli	919
Schumacher	906

SHUTOUTS

Mathewson	83
Marichal	52
Hubbell	36
Wiltse	29
Schumacher	29
Tesreau	27
McGinnity	26
Taylor	21
Fitzsimmons	21
Antonelli	21
Perry	21

BASES ON BALLS

Schumacher	902
Mathewson	839
Hubbell	725
Marichal	690
Fitzsimmons	670
Ames	620
Perry	581
Tesreau	572
Antonelli	548
Taylor	535

HITS ALLOWED

Mathewson	4118
Hubbell	3461
Marichal	3081
Fitzsimmons	2607
Schumacher	2483
Perry	2061
McGinnity	1973
Barr	1863
Wiltse	1848
Taylor	1799

COMPLETE GAMES
(SINCE 1910)

Mathewson	434
Hubbell	245
Marichal	244
Fitzsimmons	150
Schumacher	133
Perry	125
Tesreau	124
Jansen	105
Marquard	100
Nehf	95

GIANTS ALL-TIME BATTING LEADERS

GAMES

Mays	2857
Ott	2730
McCovey	2256
Terry	1721
Jackson	1656
Doyle	1615
Davenport	1501
Lockman	1485
Tiernan	1474
G. J. Burns	1362

BATTING AVG

Terry	341
G. S. Davis	335
Connor	334
Van Haltren	323
Youngs	322
Frisch	321
Lindstrom	318
Tiernan	317
Ewing	315
E. Meusel	314

AT-BATS

Mays	10,477
Ott	9456
McCovey	7214
Terry	6428
Jackson	6086
Doyle	5995
Tiernan	5910
Lockman	5584
J. Moore	5427
G. J. Burns	5311

RUNS

Mays	2011
Ott	1859
Tiernan	1312
Terry	1120
McCovey	1113
Van Haltren	982
Connor	939
Doyle	906
G. J. Burns	877
G. S. Davis	844

HITS

Mays	3187
Ott	2876
Terry	2193
McCovey	1974
Tiernan	1875
Jackson	1768
Doyle	1751
J. Moore	1615
Van Haltren	1592
Lockman	1571

DOUBLES

Mays	504
Ott	488
Terry	374
McCovey	308
Jackson	291
Doyle	275
G. J. Burns	267
J. Moore	258
Tiernan	248
Connor	240

TRIPLES

Tiernan	159
Mays	139
Connor	129
Doyle	117
Terry	112
Ewing	108
G. S. Davis	97
Youngs	93
Van Haltren	90
Jackson	86

HOME RUNS

Mays	646
Ott	511
McCovey	469
Cepeda	226
Thomson	189
Bonds	186
J. Clark	163
Hart	157
Mize	157
Terry	154

RUNS BATTED IN

Ott	1860
Mays	1859
McCovey	1388
Terry	1078
Jackson	929
Tiernan	852
G. S. Davis	805
Cepeda	767
Kelly	761
Doyle	728

STOLEN BASES

G. J. Burns	334
Mays	332
Doyle	271
Devlin	264
Bonds	263
Murray	231
Frisch	224
Merkle	192
Snodgrass	190
Youngs	153

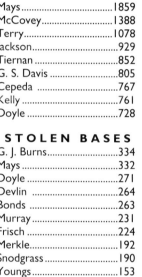

151

BIBLIOGRAPHY

Alexander, Charles. *John McGraw*. New York: Penguin, 1988.

Durso, Joseph. *The Days of Mr. McGraw*. Englewood Cliffs, N.J.: Prentice-Hall, 1969.

Einstein, Charles. *Willie's Time*. New York: Lippincott, 1979.

Fleming, G. H. *The Unforgettable Season*. New York: Holt, Rhinehart, Winston, 1981.

Frommer, Harvey. *New York City Baseball*. New York: Macmillan, 1980.

Graham, Frank. *McGraw of the Giants*. New York: Putnam, 1944.

Hodges, Russ. *My Giants*. New York: Doubleday, 1963.

Hynd, Noel. *Giants of the Polo Grounds: The Glorious Times of Baseball's New York Giants*. New York: Doubleday, 1988.

King, Joe. *The San Francisco Giants*. Englewood Cliffs, N.J.: Prentice-Hall, 1958.

Mays, Willie, and Lou Sahadi. *Say Hey: The Autobiography of Willie Mays*. New York: Pocket Books, 1988.

Robinson, Ray. *The Home Run Heard 'Round the World*. New York: HarperCollins, 1991.

Schoor, Gene. *Willie Mays, Modest Champion*. New York: Putnam, 1960.

AUTOGRAPH PAGE

INDEX

PHOTOGRAPHY CREDITS

All photography by David M. Spindel with the following exceptions:

Courtesy Alex's MVP Cards, New York: p. 149;
AP/Wide World Photos: pp. 83, 88, 134, 141;
National Baseball Library, Cooperstown, N.Y.: pp. 19 top left, 20, 24, 27 top, 29, 30 bottom, 31, 32, 37, 41, 42 top, 45, 48, 51, 52, 55, 56, 58, 64, 66, 67, 73, 76 left, 90, 93, 96, 105, 111, 115, 124 right, 138 bottom right;
© 1992 Photofile: pp. 122 left, 136, 139;
Courtesy San Francisco Giants: pp. 117, 121;
UPI/Bettmann: pp. 59, 63, 74, 80, 100, 106, 108, 118, 127.